# CREATIVE
# GIFT WRAPPING

# CREATIVE GIFT WRAPPING

## GILL DICKINSON

 Reader's Digest

THE READER'S DIGEST ASSOCIATION, INC.
Pleasantville, New York/Montreal

# CREATIVE GIFT WRAPPING

First printing in paperback November 2005

A READER'S DIGEST BOOK

Produced by Tucker Slingsby Ltd

Copyright © 1997 Tucker Slingsby Ltd
Copyright © 2005 Tucker Slingsby Ltd paperback edition

Library of Congress Cataloging in Publication Data

Dickinson, Gill.
     Creative gift wrapping / Gill Dickinson
       p.   cm.
     Includes index.
     ISBN 0-89577-962-5 (hardcover)
     ISBN 0-7621-0647-6 (paperback)
     1.Gift wrapping.       I. Title
TT870.D47    1997
745.54—dc21                97-3432

Photography by Debbie Patterson and Andrew Sydenham
Illustrations by Kate Simunek
Project Editor: Sally Harding
Art Director: Prue Bucknall

Printed in Thailand
Color reproduction by Bright Arts Graphics, Singapore

1 3 5 7 9 10 8 6 4 2 (hardcover)
1 3 5 7 9 10 8 6 4 2 (paperback)

# CONTENTS

# INTRODUCTION

Throughout the year there are many occasions when gifts are given and exchanged. It may be a festival such as Christmas or Easter, or a birthday or wedding celebration. A beautifully wrapped gift will always give extra pleasure to the recipient.

Many store-bought papers, cards, and tags are expensive and unoriginal, making your gift look uninspiring. Handmade papers, cards, and tags are the ideal solution. Even the easiest designs—a pretty torn-paper gift wrap and tag, or a simple stamped envelope or card—will look original and effective.

In the following pages, you will find exciting projects that are divided into different occasions, with themes, techniques, and finishing touches to suit everyone. For children to make and receive, there are simple projects such as cut-paper decorations and rubber stamping designs. For those in a hurry there are "instant" finishing touches which make all the difference in no time at all. And for those who want to create something really special, the découpage, stenciling, and paper-piercing projects will provide ideal inspiration. The illustrated directory at the back of the book enables you, at a glance, to review all the techniques and finishing touches included in the book.

Creative gift wrapping doesn't depend on buying new materials every time you need to wrap a gift. It is always worthwhile keeping a selection of old boxes, cards and wrapping paper, plus scraps of fabric, ribbon, buttons, and sequins. Damaged boxes can be sprayed with paint, decorated with stencils or découpage motifs, and recycled as stunning new designs. Greeting cards and wrapping paper that have already been used can be cut up to make tags and colorful motifs.

Keep an eye out when on vacation or strolling in the park for the wonderful selection of natural objects that you can collect. Shells, driftwood, feathers, pine cones, and leaves, twigs, flowers, and berries can all be used to add an extra finishing touch to your present. You will be surprised how the simplest and least

expensive idea can be the most effective. Try spattered brown paper, string, and a pressed gilded leaf on your gift, or paper decorated with relief paint, tied with raffia, and finished with a tiny bunch of fresh flowers.

Often a gift will dictate the shape of the wrapping: a round tin, bottle, or book for example. This doesn't mean that you have to make a conventional package. Try crepe paper for a round parcel. It is not only soft and pliable but fast and easy to use. Corrugated cardboard gives a handsome textural finish when wrapped around a bottle. A mundane-looking book-shaped package can be given a fresh look by adding a contrasting band of decorated paper to it. And remember that using a decorated box is both a stylish way to disguise a gift and a great way of wrapping an awkward shape.

Some gift-wrapping techniques take a little longer than others, but the end results are even more rewarding. Special boxes, bags, cards and tags will be kept as keepsakes for years to come—a handmade wedding card will always be treasured and a Christmas stocking will be brought out each year to be filled with goodies. Pretty gift bags made from colored muslin or silk and tied with silver or gold gauze ribbons can be used for many occasions and can be personalized with motifs or initials to suit the lucky recipient.

Don't reserve your gift-wrapping skills just for special occasions. When you give a small inexpensive gift to say "thank you" or "get well soon," the presentation is even more important and a handmade wrapping shows you have taken time and trouble. Homemade cookies in a hand-stenciled box or a potted plant wrapped with particular care are examples of how everyday gifts can be made memorable.

Be resourceful and original and remember that the unexpected is always appealing.

7

# GETTING
# STARTED

In this section you'll find advice on choosing the
best raw materials for great gift wrap from paper
and paint to ribbons and bows. Find out how to
wrap gifts of all shapes and sizes perfectly and
how to make your own envelopes, boxes, and bags.

# TOOLS AND EQUIPMENT

Most of the necessary tools and equipment for gift wrapping you probably already have at hand. Aside from these basics, make sure that you have a flat work surface and good light.

The handy checklist on the left outlines everything you will need to accomplish the quick and easy techniques and finishing touches in the special occasions section. More details are given below and on the next page.

## FOR DECORATIVE TECHNIQUES

Some decorative paper techniques, such as torn, cut, or pierced motifs, require little more than the chosen gift paper and cutting or piercing tools; for others you will need paint, chalk, or rubber stamps.

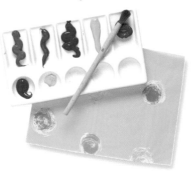

*GENERAL PAINTS* Ready-mixed poster paints are the most economical paints to use for decorating gift paper, tags, or cards. Poster colors have a matte finish and can be used in their purchased consistency or can be watered down for effects such as spattering.

Gouache, an opaque version of watercolor paint, is, like poster paint, water-soluble. Unlike poster paint, it has the advantage of coming in a tube in a thicker consistency. Gouache is more expensive than poster paint.

Spray paint is useful for covering old boxes and as a base for decorative designs. It has an acrylic base, is quite quick drying, and should always be applied in a well-ventilated space.

*SPECIALTY PAINTS* As an alternative to poster paint or gouache, powdered paints can be used. These are mixed with water and have a slightly chalky appearance. Where metallic paints are called for, gilding powders mixed with the required medium are especially effective.

Many other types of specialty paints can be found in craft stores. Two of the more useful ones are plastic relief paint and glitter glue. Plastic relief paint comes in a range of colors, as well as metallic shades. It is applied directly from the tube and adds both color and texture to your decoration. Glitter glue is also applied to the paper directly from the tube; it is a neat way to use glitter—without the mess of spreading loose glitter from a bottle onto a gluey surface.

The most unexpected ingredient for decorating paper is household bleach. Mixed with water, it can be used in place of paints for creating bleached-out designs on tissue or crepe paper (see pages 72 and 73).

*PAINTBRUSHES* An ordinary paintbrush is suitable for gilding (see page 38) and for bleached patterns. A short bristled stencil brush is best for stenciling, and an old toothbrush for spattering.

*CHALKS* For chalk designs on paper you will need chalk in a range of colors and a chalk fixative to prevent the finished design from smudging.

*RUBBER STAMPS* These provide a quick and easy way of decorating paper. You will find stamps in craft or artist supply stores. Ink can be taken from an ink pad or applied with a roller.

*READY-MADE DECORATIONS* Tiny decorations, such as confetti, self-adhesive decals, or flat sequins, can be added to your tags, cards, or gift paper.

## FOR CUTTING, PUNCHING, AND PIERCING

These tools are used both for creating decorations and for cutting papers and motif templates.

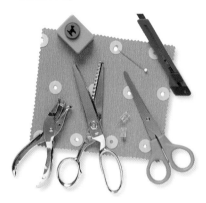

*SCISSORS* It is handy to have paper scissors in at least two sizes. Some motif templates, shaped parcels, or découpage cutouts have quite intricate edges that are easier to cut with small blades, while most other jobs can be done with large- or medium-sized scissors. Pinking shears are useful for cutting quick decorative edges.

*OTHER TOOLS* Stencils are best cut with a craft or utility knife, on a cutting mat (see page 66). You can also use a craft knife and cutting mat for cutting out homemade envelopes and boxes. Remember to use the knife with care and always use a metal ruler when cutting straight lines.

A tape measure is useful for checking the size of wrapping paper or the length of ribbon required, and a ruler is needed for scoring foldlines when making envelopes and boxes.

A paper hole punch is well worth purchasing if you intend to make a number of gift tags. A hole punch can also be used for decorative effects.

For pierced paper designs, use a posterboard pin, which has a head that is easy to hold. An ordinary sewing needle can be used for finer holes.

## FOR TRANSFERRING DESIGNS

To transfer the motifs from the Template Library (see pages 112–127), you need a pencil, a felt-tipped pen, and tracing paper. Masking tape can be handy for securing your chosen paper to a window when transferring traced motifs. The templates can be used as stencils or as guides for tracing. Either way, you can use thin cardboard or stiff paper. You also need thin cardboard for making tassels and some types of bows (see pages 20, 21, and 23).

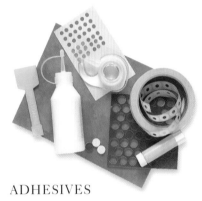

## ADHESIVES

Double-sided adhesive tape can be applied "invisibly" and so is ideal for sealing the paper overlaps of wrapped gifts. Masking tape is neccessary for masking out stripes when stenciling.

A strong liquid glue (PVA) is best for attaching cutouts. It dries clear and can be diluted and used as a sealant to cover a box decorated with découpage. Where such a strong glue is not required or where it may discolor the paper dye, a glue stick should be used. Use a fabric glue for attaching fabric cutouts to paper.

Two specialty adhesives that are useful are self-adhesive hole reinforcements for the holes on tags, and sticky foam mounts, which are thick pads with adhesive on both sides. Foam pads are used for creating a relief effect when applying cutouts to cards or tags.

# PAPERS

Before you buy or begin decorating gift paper, think about the present you want to wrap. Irregularly shaped packages are much easier to wrap in soft papers such as tissue or crepe. Thicker papers can be used to wrap a gift in a box. Save stiff, expensive handmade paper for making cards and tags or a band to go around a gift. That way one sheet can be used to decorate many gifts.

While specialty paper stores are a treasure trove of ideas, don't neglect business stationery stores, where a wide range of reasonably priced papers can be bought. If you build up a stock of paper, try to store the sheets flat. If space is scarce, they can be rolled, but take care not to damage the ends.

*MARBLED PAPER* When choosing papers for decorating, it is not necessary to select only solid-colored ones. Marbled papers, for instance, look quite stunning made into paper roses (see page 68), or used as shaped cutouts on tags or cards (see page 66).

*PURCHASED GIFT WRAP* Most easily available, store-bought gift wrapping paper comes in a wide range of colors and designs and is a great standby when time is short. Your own finishing touches—bows, tags, flowers, and other decorations—will give purchased paper an individual look.

items. White tissue paper is useful as an underwrapping for see-through gift papers. Both chalked (see page 48) and bleached (see page 72) patterns will work well on tissue paper, but tissue comes in various qualities and some will respond better to bleaching than others so it is important to experiment on scraps first.

*BROWN PAPER* Brown wrapping paper is a good neutral base for many decorations. Brown paper also makes useful pleated stuffing (see page 87). Similar "industrial" papers are also available in a range of dyed colors that retain the characteristic faint stripes and shiny surface. These colored papers make a handsome base for a number of quick paint techniques. They are inexpensively priced and, decorated, suitable for most occasions.

*HANDMADE PAPERS* Generally more expensive than manufactured papers, handmade papers are sometimes worth the expense if the gift is a special one. Handmade papers usually have a wonderful texture and come in unusual colors and designs. The examples above are just a tiny sampling of the handmade papers available.

*TISSUE PAPER* This lightweight paper comes in a wide range of colors. Since it is very pliable, tissue paper is ideal for wrapping odd shapes or fragile

*CORRUGATED PAPER* Adding colored corrugated paper to a paper decoration will introduce a lively contrast of

texture. Corrugated paper is also an attractive and protective wrap for bottles or glass jars, and can be used to produce unusual flatpacks or envelopes (see pages 27 and 24). Corrugated paper can also be used for sturdy gift tags and cards—ideal for presents that have to be mailed.

*CREPE PAPER* Pliable crepe paper is perfect for wrapping round shapes (see page 16) or for making little gift bags (see page 80). Double-sided crepe paper with a different color on each side is now available. Look for it in specialty paper stores. A mock crepe, which has the texture of real crepe paper but is not stretchy, is also available and is a good choice if you want a firm paper with a crepe finish.

*FOIL PAPER* Metallic papers are usually associated with Christmas gift wraps, but they can also be combined with other papers in cut-paper decorations to act as small highlights. Stiff metallic paper is also good for making an eye-catching envelope.

*TRANSPARENT PAPERS* Cellophane and tracing papers make unusual gift wraps. Cellophane, which some specialty paper stores stock in a range of colored or patterned versions, makes attractive wrapping for fresh and dried flowers and can be used to make small bags that will show off colorful contents (see page 29). Tracing paper is an interesting base for découpage gift paper (see page 61). Envelopes made from thick tracing paper are easily decorated by slipping colorful papers inside (see page 62).

*CONSTRUCTION PAPER* Stiff colored paper like this is usually not pliable enough to wrap boxes neatly, but it is ideal for cutting out motifs. It is also useful for making cones (see page 29), which are a great way to wrap candies or party favors and can be used for colorful table decorations. Construction paper also provides a good base for tags and cards and makes crisp, sturdy envelopes for cards and small gifts. In addition, this paper takes rubber and vegetable stamp motifs well.

## REUSING PAPER

Always save scraps of pretty paper and greeting cards. They can be used for cut- and torn-paper projects, for making tags, and for decorating cards and envelopes. And if you want to try out a decorative paper technique but don't want to go to the expense of buying papers specially, reuse paper instead.

You will be surprised how much used paper you can collect if you put your mind to it. Brown paper bags, old newspapers and magazines, junk mail, and used gift-wrapping papers all have potential. They can be covered with stenciled or stamped motifs, spattered or sprayed with paint, decorated with cutouts, or simply used for découpage on your store-bought base paper.

Any defects in used papers will be largely covered by the new surface decorations. But there are two other ways to disguise the fact that the papers are worn. First, lightweight papers, such as tissue paper, can be ironed to remove creases. Second, used papers can be deliberately crumpled and creased all over and then decorated on top of this appealing crinkled texture (see example on page 104).

Using recyclable papers for decorative paper techniques is especially good when working with children. The recipient will be so pleased with a personalized gift that he or she won't notice the recycled paper!

# WRAPPING GIFTS

Take time to decide on the best way to present your gift. First of all, consider the size of the present. If it will fit in a box, this should be your first choice. Boxes are easy to wrap neatly and you also have the option of working decorative techniques directly onto the box as well as wrapping it in paper. The other advantage of putting your present in a box is that it protects the contents and keeps secret the shape of the object within (see page 27 for making a box and page 26 for recycling old boxes).

If you decide on using a box, consider whether a square, oblong, or round box, or a tube, will work best. Instructions for wrapping these shapes follow. Square or oblong boxes can be wrapped in most types of gift paper, but round boxes and tubes are easiest to wrap in a soft, pliable paper such as crepe paper, tissue paper, or cellophane.

Some popular gifts, such as books and bottles, do not really require a box. A book can be wrapped in just the same way as an oblong box, and a suggestion for an interesting way to wrap a bottle is given on page 17. Another very popular gift is a house-plant. To make your potted plant stand out from the crowd, use the wrapping idea on page 17.

For other ways of presenting your gifts—in flatpacks, cones or decorative bags—turn to pages 26–31.

## WRAPPING A SQUARE OR OBLONG BOX

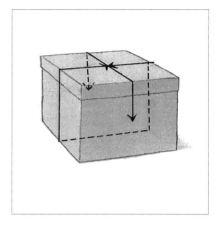

**1** To find out the size of paper you need for wrapping a square or oblong box, first measure the box. Using a tape measure, note down the width and length all around the box. Add 4 in (10 cm) to the width and 1½ in (4 cm) to the length, to give the size of the gift paper you need.

**4** Center the overlap foldline on the box. Then center the box inside the gift paper. Fold down the paper at one end so that it lies flat against the end of the box. Then crease each side flap as shown.

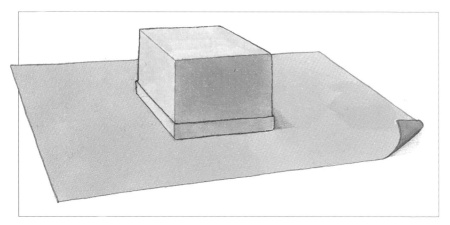

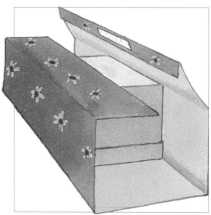

**2** Do not cut your gift paper until you are sure about the size. If in doubt, you can test the paper size (calculated in Step 1) by using a piece of newspaper of the same size, then adjust the measurements as necessary.

Once you are sure about the measurements, cut the gift paper to the correct size. Lay the paper face down on a flat, firm surface and place the box in the center of the paper with the box top facing downward.

**3** Wrap the paper around the box and fold under about 1 in (2.5 cm) along the two overlapping edges. Apply tape (double-sided is best) to the top overlap and press in place.

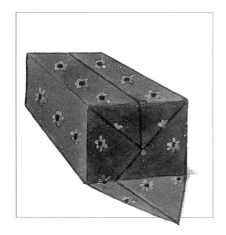

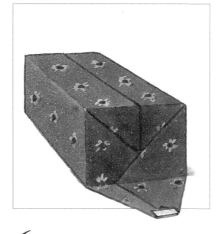

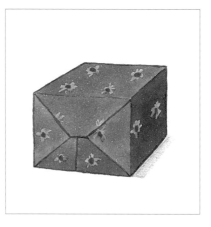

**5** Push the side flaps in toward the center of the box end, and crease the lower flap into a point.

**6** Fold the point of the flap in so that the point foldline will reach the center of the box end. Apply a piece of tape to the point. Fold up the flap and press in place.

**7** Push in the paper at the opposite end of the box, and fold in the flaps as for the first end. The box is now ready for tying with ribbon or applying other decorations.

## WRAPPING A ROUND BOX

**1** Cut a rough circle of crepe paper, or other soft paper, large enough to fit around the round box and be gathered at the top. Place the box in the center of the paper and bring the edges of the paper up to the top.

**2** Tie the gathered paper with a length of ribbon or string. If using handmade string (see page 81) as shown on the left, tie several lengths of string around the gathered paper to enhance the effect, and trim the ends. Don't pull handmade string too tightly.

## WRAPPING A TUBE

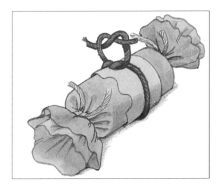

**1** Make a cardboard tube to fit around your gift, then cut a piece of crepe paper that is wide enough to fit around the tube plus a 4 in (10 cm) overlap, and long enough for two gathered ends. Cut a piece of tissue the same width as the crepe paper but a little longer. With the tissue paper inside the crepe paper, wrap the paper around the tube. Then fold under both layers at one edge and secure the folded edge with double-sided tape.

**2** Gather each end of the paper together close to the tube and tie with a length of handmade crepe paper string or ribbon.

**3** For an added decorative touch, add a band of crepe paper around the center of the tube and secure with contrasting paper string.

## WRAPPING A FLOWERPOT

Set the flowerpot in the center of a large piece of brown paper. Bring the paper up around the pot and tie with a length of string or ribbon to secure. Decorate by putting a few fresh leaves behind the bow.

## WRAPPING A BOTTLE WITH CORRUGATED PAPER

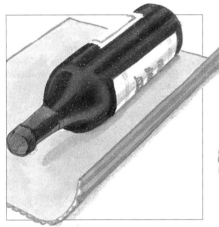

1 Lay the corrugated paper wrong side up and place the bottle on it to use as a guide for cutting. Cut the paper wide enough to fit around the bottle plus a 1½ in (4 cm) overlap, and as long as the bottle plus an additional 2 in (5 cm) to extend above the top.

2 Wrap the corrugated paper tightly around the bottle and secure the overlap in place with strong double-sided tape or glue.

3 Wrap a band of contrasting paper around the tube and secure the overlap in place with sticky tape. Tie string or ribbon around the band. To decorate, put fresh or dried leaves and flowers under the string or ribbon. Or you can make paper or ribbon flowers (see page 107) if the gift will be left unopened for some time.

# RIBBONS, TIES, AND BOWS

There is such a wide range of ribbons and colored strings now available that the choice can be bewildering. Always look for a tie or bow that will complement the color and textural qualities of your chosen paper. Notions departments are good sources for all types of fabric ribbons, wire-edged ribbons, and embroidery threads, and for more unusual and original ties you can use string, raffia, or wool. Save any ribbon or interesting ties you find or are given; even the smallest scrap of ribbon or colorful thread will be useful to attach a tag. And scraps of fabric from your work basket can also be used—net and other non-fraying fabrics make great bows. See the Directory of Finishing Touches on page 108 for more ideas, including ties you can make yourself from paper.

*PAPER AND SYNTHETIC RIBBON* Many types of narrow, flat paper and synthetic ribbons can be curled with a blunt knife to create attractive trailers.

*TWISTED-PAPER RIBBON* This type of paper ribbon can be used twisted, as it comes, or untwisted into a wide crinkled paper, wonderful for big bows.

*FABRIC RIBBON* Fabric ribbons of all descriptions are widely available, from bright tartans and checks to filmy, transparent ribbons. These ribbons can be expensive so reuse them whenever possible.

*STRING* Ordinary or decorative strings make a good finishing touch for a present intended for a man. You can wrap them round the gift several times for more impact. They can also be painted for a softer effect (see page 38).

*GROSGRAIN RIBBON* This crisp, ribbed fabric ribbon is especially suitable for wrapping around small gifts or for tying on tags. Because it is very durable, you can iron and recycle it.

*WIRE-EDGED RIBBON* This type of ribbon has thin wire woven into its selvages and so will retain whatever shape you bend it into. This makes it perfect for making bold bows.

*RAFFIA* A single strand of raffia makes a good tie for a tag or an envelope. Lots of strands used together make bows with a rustic effect (see page 20).

*YARN AND EMBROIDERY THREAD* Wool and embroidery threads are ideal for tying tags to gifts. They can also be used for tying around small gifts or for making tassels (see page 23).

## TYING A BASIC BOW

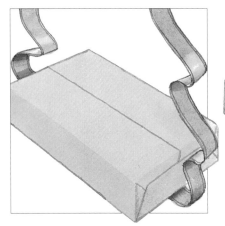

**1** To calculate how much ribbon you will need, follow these steps using a piece of string, then measure it and cut your ribbon to the same length. First lay the box upside down on the center of the ribbon.

**2** With the ribbon centered on the box, cross over the ends by passing one ribbon end over and under the other as shown.

**3** Bring the two ends around the sides of the box and turn the box over so that the top faces upward. Then pass one ribbon end over the other and under the ribbon on the box.

**4** Pull the ends of the ribbon so that it fits snuggly on the box. Then form a loop with one ribbon end.

**5** Wrap the free ribbon end around the looped end, and pull it through to form the second loop of the bow.

**6** Pull the two loops to tighten the knot at the center. Then trim the ends of the ribbon on the diagonal or cut an inverted V-shape.

## MAKING A RAFFIA BOW

**1** Cut a length of raffia long enough to tie around the center of the bow and also around the gift, and set aside. Cut a piece of cardboard the same width as the required bow size. Then, holding the group of raffia strands together as they are packaged, wrap the raffia around the cardboard a few times.

**2** Slip the raffia loops off the piece of cardboard, keeping the center of the loops very firmly pinched together.

**3** Take the strand of raffia that you cut in Step 1 and wrap it a few times around the center of the raffia loops. Knot the strand ends together at the back of the bow, and leave the long ends to attach the bow to the gift. Trim the bow ends.

## MAKING A TWISTED-PAPER RIBBON BOW

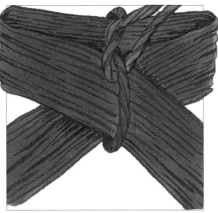

**1** Cut a length of twisted-paper ribbon four times the length of the required finished bow. Before tying the bow, open and spread wide the entire length of the paper ribbon, which comes tightly twisted together.

**2** Fold the ribbon into a bow shape as shown and tie it around the center with a length of string. Knot the string, then trim the string ends close to the knot. Cut another short length of paper ribbon. Do not open out.

**3** Cover the center of the bow with this length of paper ribbon and trim the ends of this ribbon or leave them long to use for tying the bow to the present. Trim the bow ends.

## MAKING A BOW WITH TRAILERS

**1** For the trailers, cut lengths of ribbon twice as long as the desired finished trailer length. About twice as long as the bow is ideal. The finished red satin bow on the facing page illustrates this. Set the trailers aside.

**2** Using the same ribbon, make a bow as for Steps 1 and 2 for the raffia bow on page 20, but wrapping the single strand of ribbon many times around the cardboard. Take a separate length of ribbon and tie the bow and trailers together around the center.

## MAKING A RIBBON ROSE

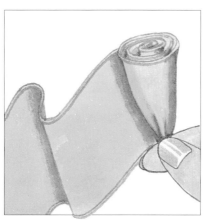

**1** Using a 20 in (50 cm) length of wire-edged ribbon, roll the ribbon a few turns, pinching the base together as you roll. Then continue rolling, but form little pleats at the base so that the top edge begins to flare out.

**2** As you near the end of the ribbon, increase the size of the pleats. Fold the end of the ribbon under, then tie the pleated base together with florists' wire.

## MAKING AN EMBELLISHED BOW

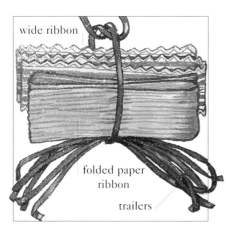

wide ribbon

folded paper ribbon

trailers

sheer ribbon

**1** Cut about 12 strands of narrow ribbon for trailers and set aside. Then fold a length of wide ribbon back and forth to form loops at both sides as shown. Take a length of twisted paper ribbon, open it up, and fold it in the same way. Place the folded ribbons and the trailers together and tie tightly around the center with a separate length of narrow ribbon.

**2** Using a sheer ribbon, tie a big bow around the center of the ribbons tied together in Step 1. Then fan out the ribbon loops to form a full circular bow, twisting them as necessary to adjust the shape. If desired, insert a paper rose in the center of the finished embellished bow. You can achieve different effects by using different types of ribbon.

## MAKING A TASSEL

**1** Cut two pieces of cardboard as long as the required length of the tassel. Place the cardboard pieces together. Wrap a generous amount of thread or narrow ribbon around the two layers of cardboard. For a thicker tassel use wool or raffia. Tie the loops together at one end with a separate length of thread.

**2** Slip the point of a pair of scissors between the two layers of cardboard at the end of the loops that is not tied, and cut through the loops. Remove the cardboard.

**3** Using a matching or contrasting thread, make a loop with one end of the thread, then wrap the thread around the head of the tassel and over the loop just made. To secure the wrapped thread, slip the end through the loop and pull both thread ends tightly to pull the loop inside the wrapping. Trim off the thread ends.

## MAKING A CUT-END BOW

**1** Cut a piece of cardboard as wide as you want the finished bow. Wind raffia, string, or ribbon around the cardboard. Slip the loops off the cardboard, keeping them pinched together. Tie firmly in the center. Cut the loops at both ends of the bow.

# ENVELOPES

Decorative envelopes are a wonderful finishing touch for the card that accompanies your gift. They can also be used as containers for congratulatory messages, gift tokens, money or checks, or even small gifts. (For instructions on how to make shaped envelopes for small gifts, see the shaped tree parcels on page 93.)

Stiff colored paper or thin cardboard are ideal for envelopes, but interesting alternatives are corrugated cardboard, metallic papers, and tracing paper. Whether you make your own envelope following the instructions given here or buy an envelope, you can decorate it with any of the techniques given in the next chapter.

## MAKING A SIMPLE ENVELOPE

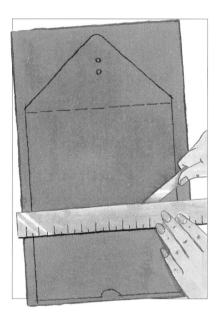

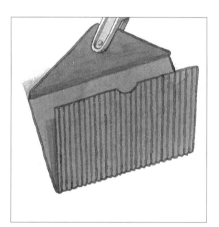

**1** Enlarge the simple envelope template (see page 112) to the desired size. Transfer the shape onto a piece of corrugated paper or other stiff paper, marking the positions for the flap holes and the foldlines. Then hold a ruler firmly in place and score the foldlines on the wrong side (the smooth side of the corrugated paper) with a dull knife or the points of a pair of scissors.

**2** Cut out the envelope shape. Crease the foldlines and fold up the envelope. Leave the sides open or glue them as desired. Punch the flap holes using a hole punch.

**3** Thread a length of string or raffia through the flap holes and wrap it around the envelope. You can thread flower and leaf cutouts (see page 74) onto the tie before making a bow.

## MAKING A WALLET ENVELOPE

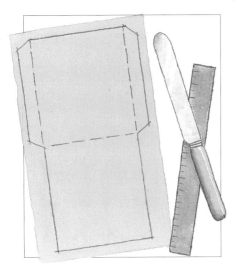

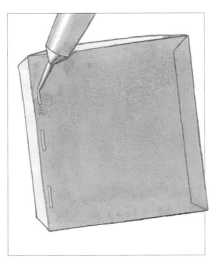

**1** Enlarge the wallet envelope template (see page 113) to any size you wish. Transfer the shape onto stiff paper and mark the positions of the foldlines. Using a ruler, score the foldlines lightly with a dull knife or the points of a pair of scissors.

**2** Cut out the envelope shape and crease the scored foldlines. Fold up the envelope and glue the side flaps on top of the back of the envelope.

**3** Decorate the front of the envelope. Then punch a hole through both layers at the top, thread ribbon through the holes, and tie a bow.

## MAKING AN ENVELOPE WITH FLAPS

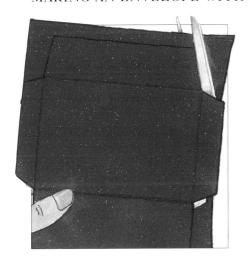

**1** Enlarge the envelope-with-flaps template (see page 113), and transfer it onto a piece of stiff paper. Mark and score the foldlines as for the wallet envelope and cut out the shape.

**2** Fold in the side flaps and glue the back of the envelope to these flaps. Then fold down the top flap. You can decorate the envelope with contrasting paper cutouts or stickers.

# BOXES AND BAGS

Ready-made gift boxes and bags are expensive to buy and it is not always possible to find the right color or shape for your gift. Try recycling a box you already have around the house by spray-painting it. The painted box can then be decorated with stenciled motifs or covered with découpage or cutout motifs. Glued-on motifs are especially useful for covering up defects on a recycled box. Alternatively, you can follow the instructions given here to make a box or bag in the card and paper of your choice. Decorated boxes and fabric bags will be treasured long after the gift inside has been eaten or forgotten so it is worth taking the time and trouble.

## SPRAY-PAINTING A USED BOX

1 Protect surfaces and do not work in an enclosed space when using spray paint. Spray one side at a time.

2 Spray-paint the outside of the lid as well. Then leave the paint on the box to dry overnight.

3 Decorate the box as desired with stenciled or spattered motifs, or with patterns, paper cutouts, or other embellishments.

## FOLDING A SQUARE TEMPLATE BOX

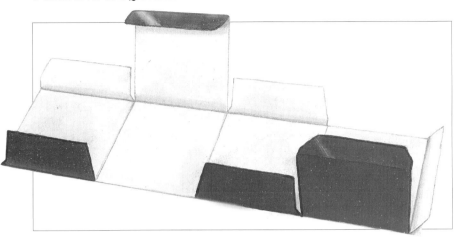 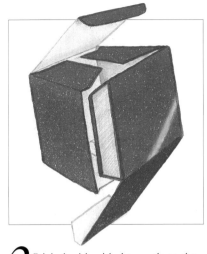

**1** Enlarge the template on page 114 as instructed. (The template can be enlarged even more for a very large box.) Transfer the shape onto a piece of thin cardboard that will fold easily. Transfer the foldline markings as well.

Before cutting out the box shape, score the foldlines on the wrong side with a dull knife or the points of a pair of scissors, using a ruler as a guide. Then cut out the box shape. Crease the cardboard along each of the foldlines.

**2** Stick double-sided tape along the side overlap. Press the box together over the tape. Fold up the side tabs at the bottom of the box and push the bottom up into place, tucking the tab straight up into the box. Finally, fold the top down, inserting the tab straight down into the box.

## FOLDING A CORRUGATED FLATPACK

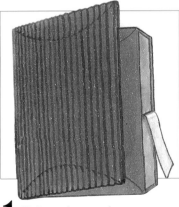  

**1** Enlarge the template on page 115, and transfer the shape onto a piece of corrugated paper or thin card. Score the foldlines on the right side. Cut out the shape. Crease along the foldlines, and stick double-sided tape along the wrong side of the overlap.

**2** Fold the flatpack together and press the overlap onto the right side of the back of the flatpack. Push in the rounded flaps at the top and bottom of the flatpack. To open the envelope, squeeze the sides together and lift the top flaps. Decorate the envelope as required.

## MAKING A PAPER GIFT BAG

**1** Select a book that is the size of the bag you require (you can stack a few books together for a larger size). Cut a piece of stiff paper that is wide enough to wrap around the book with a 1 in (2.5 cm) overlap, and as long as the required finished bag plus extra for the base and at least 1¼ in (3 cm) extra for folding down at the top. Fold the top edge of the paper to the wrong side and secure with double-sided tape to reinforce the opening.

**2** Lay the book on the wrong side of the paper, with the unfolded edge of the paper extending past the end. Wrap the paper around the book and secure the overlap with double-sided tape or glue.

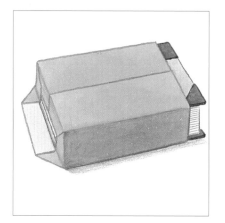

**3** Crease the four corners of the bag along the length of the edges of the book. Then fold in the paper at the base of the bag as for wrapping a box (see page 14). Secure the folded base with double-sided tape or glue.

**4** Punch two holes in the top edge of both the front and the back of the bag as shown. Make two handles by threading a length of cord or ribbon through the holes on each side, then knotting the ends to secure.

## MAKING A CELLOPHANE BAG

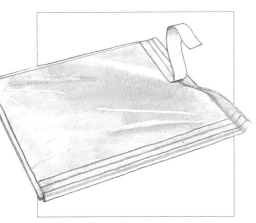
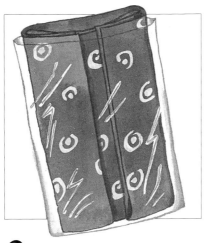

**1** Cut a cardboard template as wide as you want the finished bag to be and 1 in (2.5 cm) longer. Cut a piece of cellophane twice as wide as the cardboard plus a ¾ in (2 cm) overlap. Wrap the cellophane around the cardboard and seal the overlap together with cellophane tape. Fold up one end as shown and seal in the same way.

**2** Slip the cellophane bag off the cardboard template. Then wrap a piece of tissue paper around the gift, folding the paper to the same size as the cellophane bag. Slip the folded tissue paper inside the cellophane bag. Alternatively, small gifts can be wrapped individually in different colored tissue papers and inserted into the bag separately.

**3** To finish the decoration, tie a length of ribbon around the neck of the bag and make a bow with the ribbon ends. For an interesting finishing touch, tie two strands of narrow ribbon around the bag together, instead of just one.

## MAKING A CONE

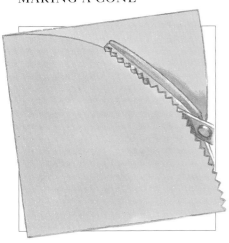
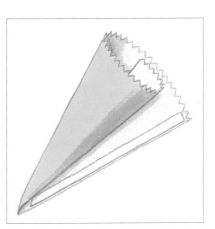

**1** Using the cone template on page 115, cut a cone shape from stiff paper. Cut the top edge with pinking shears if you wish.

**2** Roll the cone, overlapping the edges as much as necessary to achieve the desired shape, and secure with double-sided tape. Decorate with a bow, then wrap the gift in colored tissue paper and insert.

## MAKING A FABRIC BAG

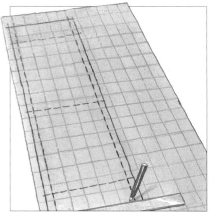

**1** For the fabric size needed see the instructions for the Christmas bag on page 98 or calculate the dimensions for your own bag and make a paper pattern. The fabric should be twice the bag length, plus 8 in (20 cm) extra for the turndown. The width should be the desired width, plus seam allowances of ½ in (1.5 cm) on each side.

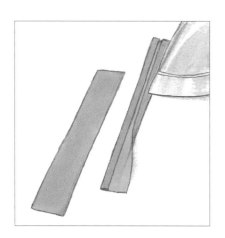

**5** For a drawstring casing, cut out two strips of fabric each as long as the width of the finished bag, by 1 in (2.5 cm) plus two ½ in (1.5 cm) seam allowances. Fold the allowances to the wrong side along both long sides of each strip and press. If you are in a hurry you can use a wide, self-edged binding tape and skip to step 7.

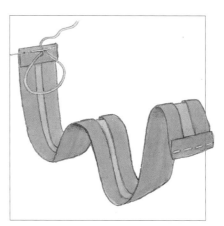

**6** Fold ½ in (1.5 cm) to the wrong side along both short ends of each casing strip and press. Then stitch along the short ends, working short, even running stitches.

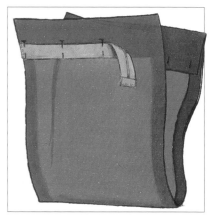

**7** With the wrong side of the casing strip facing the right side of the bag piece, pin a casing strip in the desired position below the top edge of the bag, centering it between the seam allowances. Then pin the other casing strip in place along the other end of the bag piece in a corresponding position.

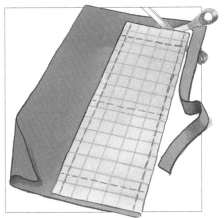

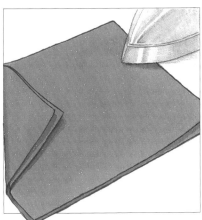

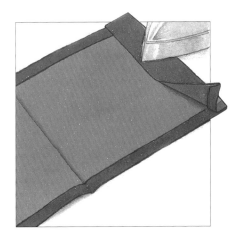

2 Cut out the single bag piece, using the pattern piece made to your own specifications or following the dimensions given on page 98. For a bag with decorations, continue to Step 3, but for a simple bag without decorations, you can skip to Step 4.

3 Fold the bag piece in half widthwise with the wrong sides together and press to mark the bottom edge of the bag. Unfold and decorate the front of the bag as desired (see the Christmas bag on page 98 for ideas).

4 Press under the seam allowances along the long sides of the bag piece. To make a quick version of the bag, pink the top edges and skip to step 9. For a bag with a decorative drawstring, press under a 4 in (10 cm) turning on both top edges.

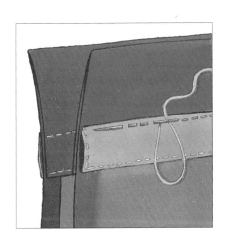

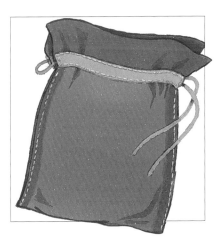

8 Hand- or machine-stitch the casing strips in place, leaving the short ends open for inserting the drawstring.

9 With wrong sides together, fold the bag piece in half widthwise. Pin and stitch the side seams with short running stitches. (Or you can machine-stitch on the inside instead.) On a bag with a casing, leave the seams open from the bottom of the casing to the top of the bag; otherwise stitch the seams to the top edge.

10 If the bag has a drawstring casing, thread a length of string, cord, or raffia through it. To thread a drawstring, pin a safety pin to one end and insert it into the casing opening. Push the pin along until it comes full circle. If the bag does not have a casing, simply put your gift inside and tie ribbon around the top.

# SPECIAL OCCASIONS

In this section you'll find inspirational gift wrapping ideas for ten different occasions, including weddings, birthdays, and, of course, Christmas. Each occasion highlights a different style, decorative technique, and finishing touch to give you as many packaging options as possible.

# CONGRATULATIONS

This catchall category of gift-giving includes anniversaries and a wide variety of other occasions, such as congratulating a friend for a special achievement—graduating from high school or college, finding a great new job, or receiving a big promotion at work.

The key to great congratulations gifts is to make the recipient feel special, to show that you appreciate his or her achievement and are marking it by sending a gift you have chosen carefully. The gift will make a stronger statement if you have also taken time and trouble with the wrapping.

Rich metals, gilts, and golds have been chosen for the gifts pictured on the left. Hand-decorated papers have been combined with metallic ribbons and gilded leaves to symbolize the importance of the milestone that has been passed.

*All the paint techniques used for these hand-decorated gift papers are quick and easy. The finished gift papers are shown here (clockwise from top right): dry-brush decoration, relief-paint dots, single brush-stroke decoration, and spattering. The natural items such as twigs and leaves added for the finishing touches are gilded as shown on pages 38 and 39. Paper leaves made with the templates on page 116 can be gilded and used as a substitute for natural ones.*

# QUICK PAINT EFFECTS

These paint effects are quick and easy to do, but the results will look as if you have labored long and hard. Before beginning any of these techniques, cover your work surface with several layers of old newspaper or other scrap paper. Make sure you cover an area larger than the size of the paper being decorated. This will not only safeguard your work surface but also ensure you can paint right up to the edges of the gift paper, making the decorating speedier and more effective.

Always test the the consistency of the paint, suitability of the brush, and the paint effect on a scrap of paper before starting on the main piece of gift paper. You should then decorate a piece of paper large enough for your gift, plus a little extra to be used for cutting a simple tag.

## MATERIALS

**For all quick paint techniques**

Plain light- or medium-weight gift paper

Old newspapers or other scrap paper for protecting work surface

**For spattering**

Poster paint in two shades

Old toothbrush

**For brush-stroke decoration**

Poster paint in one shade

Stiff, flat-ended brush

**For dry-brush decoration**

Poster paint in one shade

Stiff, flat-ended brush

**For plastic relief paint**

Plastic relief paint in one or two shades

### SPATTERING THE PAPER

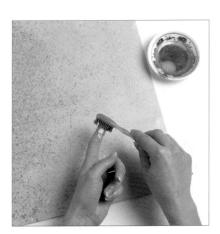

1 Smooth out the gift paper on a work surface covered with old newspaper or other scrap paper. Dip the toothbrush in paint, then spatter paint evenly across the gift paper by rubbing your finger across the bristles. Allow the spattered paint to dry for a few minutes.

2 Using a second color of paint, spatter the paper again to add highlights to the first layer of spattering. Let the paint dry completely before using the paper to wrap your gift.

## DECORATING WITH BRUSH STROKES

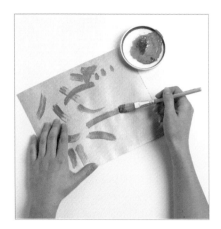

1 Choose a stiff, flat-ended brush for this technique. Test that the brush is stiff enough and that the paint is not too runny by dipping the brush in the paint and drawing it over a piece of scrap paper. Repeat until you are satisfied with the effect.

2 Dip the brush in the paint, brush off any excess onto scrap paper, and make a short stroke on the gift paper. Continuing in this way, cover the paper at random with widely spaced, short, curved strokes.

## CREATING PATTERNS WITH A DRY BRUSH

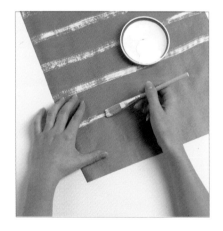

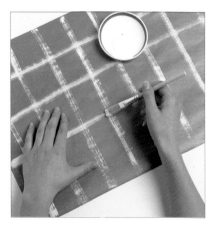

1 Test the paint as for the single brush-stroke technique above. Then apply vertical stripes about 5 in (13 cm) apart from edge to edge of the gift paper. Let the paint dry for a few minutes.

2 Dip the brush again and apply horizontal stripes across the vertical stripes. This is just one example of the type of simple pattern that can be made quickly with a dry, stiff brush. Experiment with others on scrap paper, then design your own unique gift wrapping.

## USING PLASTIC RELIEF PAINT

1 Try making small dots with plastic relief paint on a piece of scrap paper. Practice until you can squeeze the tube gently enough to make little dots without smudging the paint. Try out other simple motifs.

2 Cover the entire sheet of gift paper with small dots of paint. Allow the paint to dry completely. You can use a second paint color to fill in the spaces between the first dots to give a richer effect. See page 105 of the Directory for an example of a paper decorated in two colors.

## GILT DECORATIONS

Gilding natural objects adds a special finish to their natural beauty. The techniques shown here for gilding twigs and leaves can also be applied to many other natural objects, including berries, twigs, cones, feathers, and acorns.

Be sure to protect your work surface with old newspapers or other scrap paper before beginning the gilding. Once finished, the gilded decorations can simply be slipped in place under the ribbon on your gift. Alternatively, they can be glued to the front of an accompanying card or tag so that they can be kept as a memento of the occasion.

### MATERIALS

**For decoration**

Poster paint in two or three metallic colors

Paintbrush

Glitter glue

White plastic relief paint

Old newspapers or other scrap paper for protecting work surface

**For ribbon or string**

String of any thickness

Thick twisted paper ribbon

**For twigs**

Thoroughly dried twigs

String

Scissors

**For leaves**

Dried leaves and/or brown paper

Paper template

Scissors

### PAINTING PAPER RIBBON AND STRING

1 Lay the paper ribbon on a protected surface. Apply strokes of metallic paint at intervals all along the ribbon, then leave to dry.

2 Gild string in the same way as paper ribbon, but apply the paint along the entire length of the string and leave to dry.

### GILDING TWIGS

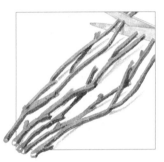 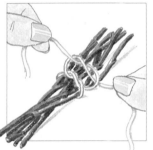 

1 Collect small twigs and leave them for a few days to dry thoroughly. Then select six or seven twigs, and cut them into similar lengths.

2 Tie the trimmed twigs together around the center with a length of fine string, and cut the string ends close to the knot.

3 Cover the twigs, and the string as well, with metallic paint. Stick the finished twig "posy" under the string tied around your gift.

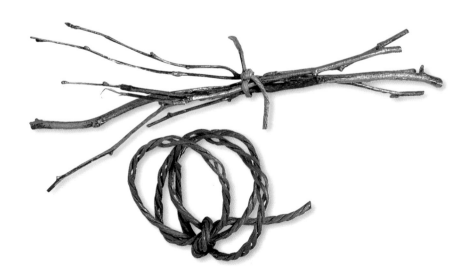

## DECORATING PRESSED AND PAPER LEAVES

**1** Collect leaves, selecting flat, well-shaped ones. Place the leaves between sheets of old newspaper, and pile books on top. Leave for a few days to dry and flatten.

**2** Alternatively, cut paper leaves from brown wrapping paper, using the templates on page 116, or using a real leaf as your template.

**3** Using one of the colors of metallic paint, decorate the pressed or paper leaves with random brush strokes. Let dry.

**4** Using a contrasting metallic paint, again decorate the leaves with random brush strokes and let dry completely.

**5** Streak the leaves with glitter glue, smudging it with your forefinger to soften the effect. Let the glue dry.

**6** As a final, optional, embellishment you can apply beads of plastic relief paint to the leaves, positioning them at random.

# WEDDING

Awedding day is one of the most eagerly anticipated celebrations. While the engaged couple and their families are taking so much care to ensure the day goes smoothly, right down to the smallest details of corsages and boutonnieres, it is only fair that you put a little extra effort into the presentation of your gift.

In addition, you may find the wedding gifts are put on display during the festivities. When the bride and groom are inundated with so many packages and presents, an individually wrapped gift is sure to stand out from the crowd.

The color palettes used for the gifts shown on the left reflect the colors used most frequently for brides' and bridesmaids' dresses—cream, white, and pastels—combined with soft net bows. The papers are embellished with golden roses and hearts, and the gifts accessorized with real and paper roses to make truly romantic gift wrapping.

*The lacy effect of pierced paper is ideal for wedding gifts. See the following pages for how to make the pierced gift paper, pierced tags and cards, net bows, and bonbonnieres shown here. The stenciled heart and flower papers are made in the same way as the paper on pages 66 and 67, but using the templates on page 121. To make the wired-ribbon roses on the two large presents, see page 22 and for the crepe paper rose on the small package, turn to page 68.*

41

# PIERCED PAPER

Since applying pierced patterns to gift paper will take a little more time than other creative gift-wrapping techniques, it is a special effect best suited to gifts that are planned well in advance. The piercing will weaken the paper a little, so choose a strong, light- to medium-weight paper that is soft enough to wrap with. A smooth texture and a pastel color will best show up the relief of the pierced holes.

How close to work the holes and the needle size for piercing depends on the paper and the chosen pattern (for Wedding templates see pages 116 and 117). Make a few sample swatches and choose the most effective needle size and hole spacing. Note that the holes are pierced from the wrong side of the paper. This makes the pierced pattern more visible on the right side.

## MAKING GIFT PAPER

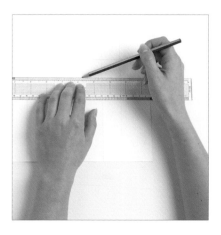

**1** Determine the size of paper you will need to wrap your gift and cut the paper to this size (see pages 14 and 15). Using a pencil and a ruler, lightly draw a 1¼ in (3 cm) square grid on the wrong side of the gift paper.

## MATERIALS

### For piercing
Well-padded surface

Needle or posterboard pin

### For transferring designs
Pencil

Ruler

Tracing paper

Stiff paper for template

Scissors

### For gift paper
Medium-weight white or pastel paper

### For tag or card
Medium-weight white or pastel paper

Hole punch

Narrow satin ribbon

Scrap of contrasting paper for tiny heart

Glue

## MAKING A TAG OR CARD

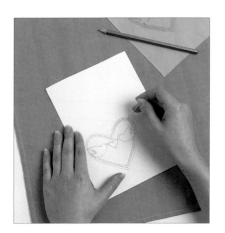

**1** Transfer the doves-and-heart tag design on page 116 onto the wrong side of the tag paper. Then lay the tag paper on a well-padded surface with the wrong side of the paper facing upward. Pierce evenly spaced holes along the pencil lines as for Step 2 of the pierced gift paper (see above right). Then cut out the tag shape.

**2** Cut a tiny heart from a contrasting paper the same size as the little pierced heart between the doves and glue it to the right side of the tag on top of the pierced heart. Use a hole punch to cut a hole at the center top of the heart, and tie on a length of narrow ribbon. Do not pierce a hole if you want to make a card.

2 Lay the paper on a well-padded
surface with the wrong side
facing upward. Make sure the needle
will not go through the padding and
damage the work surface. Pierce the
grid pattern with a needle, making
about 8 evenly spaced holes per
1 in (2.5 cm).

3 Trace a small heart (see page 117
for template) onto tracing paper.
Transfer the shape to a piece of stiff
paper and cut out. (See page 112 for
detailed template instructions.)

4 Lay the cutout heart inside a
grid square, and draw around it.
Using a pencil, lightly draw a heart in
this way inside alternate grid squares,
then pierce the hearts as for the grid.

3 To make a wedding card, cut a
card backing 7 in by 10 in (18 cm
by 24 cm) and fold it in half widthwise.
Then unfold it and transfer the card
border design to the wrong side of the
front of the card using the illustration
on page 117 as a positioning guide for
the little hearts and the double lines.
Pierce the design.

4 To complete the card, glue the
pierced-paper tag from Step 2 to
the center front of the card. To
personalize the card, you can design
your own pierced motifs using outlines
from pages 116 and 117 or create
designs of your own to suit the
personalities of the happy couple.

# NET DECORATIONS

Net does not fray easily, so it can be cut to any width or shape to make ribbon, bows, and bonbonnieres. Confetti-filled bows are made without any sewing, as the net retains its shape once creased. If you do not have any confetti or pressed flowers, try using tiny bits of colorful torn tissue or crepe paper for the filling.

Net decorations are usually associated with weddings, but they could just as effectively be made in bright colors for a little girl's birthday or in pastels for baby presents.

## MATERIALS

**For net bow**

Fine, soft net

Scissors

Confetti or pressed flower petals for filling

Tape measure

Glue

**For bonbonniere**

12 in (30 cm) square of cream or pink net

12 in (30 cm) square of cream organdy

Narrow ribbon

Scissors

Candy-coated almonds or other hard-coated or wrapped candies

Small bridal or wedding-cake decorations or tiny dried flowers for decorating ribbon (optional)

Glue (optional)

## MAKING A CONFETTI-FILLED BOW

1  Cut a strip of net about 10 in (25 cm) wide, and long enough to fit around the gift box and form a generous bow (see page 19 for how to measure ribbon).

2  Sprinkle the confetti or pressed flower petals along the center third of the net strip; do not overfill.

3  Fold first one side of the net, then the other, to the center, over the filling. Press the folds down with your hands. The filling will be caught in place by the net.

4  Tie the folded and filled net strip around the gift box and form a generous bow with the long ends.

5  Trim each end of the confetti-filled net ribbon to the desired length.

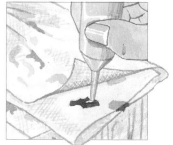

6  Insert a few more pieces of confetti or petals inside the ends, then dot two or three pieces near each end with glue to secure.

## MAKING A BONBONNIERE

**1** Cut a circle of net about 9–10 in (23–25 cm) in diameter. If desired, cut scallops around the edge to soften the finished effect of the ruffled edge.

**2** Cut a second circle the same size as the net circle but from the organdy. Again, scallop the edge of the fabric to soften the effect, if you wish.

**3** Lay the net circle on a flat surface. If desired, sprinkle some confetti on top of the net. Place the organdy circle on top of the net, aligning the raw edges.

**4** Place candy-coated almonds of the desired color in the center of the fabric circles. (Other hard or wrapped candies can be used instead.)

**5** Gather the edges of the fabric layers together over the candy, and tie in place with a length of narrow satin ribbon.

**6** You can stick a little dried flower rose onto the ribbon, or decorate the ends by gluing tiny wedding-cake decorations onto the ribbon.

# NEW BABY

The first announcement that a baby is on the way will get people planning the perfect present. It may be an exquisite, hand-knitted shawl, a soft, cuddly toy, or some luxury to pamper the mother-to-be. The baby shower is a time to get together and talk and a way of making sure that the new arrival has everything he or she could possibly need. Whether your gift is practical or luxurious, wrap it with loving care.

For the gifts shown here, tissue in bright shades is muted to pastel by the application of chalk designs. It is easy to build patterns of stripes and plaids, as is demonstrated on the pages that follow. You can choose any colors, but traditional blues, pinks, and yellows will always look good. Chain dolls, just like those you made as a child, are a cute addition and will provide a delightful topic for conversation at the baby shower.

*A baby gift or a posy of fresh flowers wrapped in one of these unusual chalked tissue papers will delight any mother-to-be. Make the papers as explained on pages 48 and 49, wrap your gift, then add grosgrain ribbons for a sharp contrast to the chalky surfaces. Crisp, white paper dolls or animal silhouette tags are the perfect finishing touch (see pages 50 and 51). For an alternative tissue wrapping for baby presents, try the delicate bleached tissue on pages 72 and 73.*

47

# CHALKED PAPER

Chalk and tissue combine beautifully to create an irresistible gift paper. The sharp tissue colors are tempered into cool pastels by the addition of chalked patterns. The designs you can try with this technique are endless, but the simple ones shown here are just as effective as more ornate swirls or shapes.

When chalking your tissue paper, make sure you have enough tissue to cover your gift with a little left over for making tags or cards (see page 50). It is essential to spray the completed chalk patterns with a fixative before wrapping the paper. Make sure you are working in a well-ventilated room when spraying fixative.

## MATERIALS

**For chalking**

Chalk in a selection of colors

Chalk fixative

Fabric remnants and a large piece of smooth, white scrap paper for padding the work surface

**For gift paper**

Tissue paper in desired color

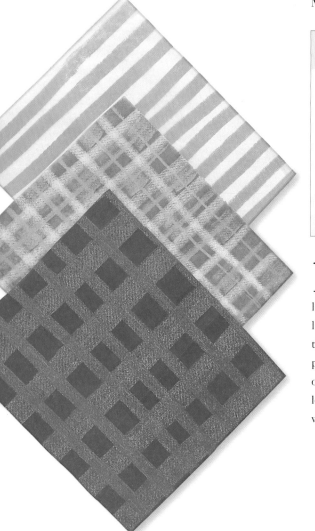

## MAKING SIMPLE STRIPES

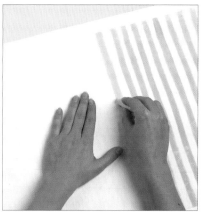

1 To create a soft surface to work on, cover your work area with two layers of fabric remnants and then a large piece of plain scrap paper. Lay the sheet of tissue on top of the scrap paper and smooth it out. Break a piece of chalk so it is roughly 1 in (2.5 cm) long and use the side of the chalk to work stripes gently across the tissue.

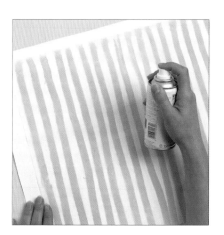

2 Don't worry if your stripes are not completely straight and even. That is the charm of handmade papers. Working in a well-ventilated room, spray the finished tissue paper with chalk fixative and leave to dry for several minutes.

## MAKING A SIMPLE CHECK PATTERN

**1** Prepare the work surface as for Step 1 of simple stripes (see previous page). Then lay a sheet of tissue paper on the padded surface. Break off a piece of chalk to the desired width of the stripe. Use the side of the chalk to draw horizontal stripes on the paper. Cover the whole sheet of tissue.

**2** Using the desired width of chalk, draw vertical stripes over the horizontal ones to form the checks. When the chalking is complete, spray with chalk fixative in a well-ventilated room and leave to dry for a few minutes.

## MAKING A PLAID PATTERN

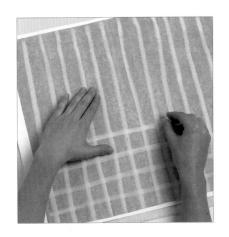

**1** Begin a plaid design by drawing horizontal lines crossed by vertical lines as for the simple check pattern in Steps 1 and 2 above, but use the end of the piece of chalk and not the wide, side edge.

**2** Using a contrasting color chalk draw narrow horizontal lines between the horizontal lines already drawn. Then, in the same way, draw narrow vertical lines between the vertical lines already drawn.

**3** With another contrasting color of chalk, draw squares at spaced intervals on the existing pattern. Working in a well-ventilated room, spray the finished design to fix the chalk. Leave to dry for a few minutes.

## MATERIALS

**For tag**

Scrap of tissue paper

Stiff white paper

Textured fabric

Lightweight paper

Chalk fixative

Scissors

Glue

Chalk in a selection of colors

Hole punch

Narrow grosgrain ribbon

**For chain motif**

Pencil

Tracing paper

Thin cardboard

Scissors

Lightweight white paper

Double-sided tape

# CHALKED TAGS

To make matching tags, try out the patterns for papers on the previous pages on small pieces of tissue, using a selection of contrasting chalks and a variety of tissue colors. For a different effect, try drawing some of the patterns with the tissue laid directly on a textured surface, such as a loose-weave fabric. Spray the swatches you have made with fixative and keep them as a handy library of designs, or use them to make unique tags as you need them. When using spray fixative work in a well-ventilated room.

## MAKING A TAG

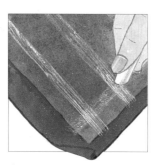

**1** Lay a piece of tissue paper directly on the textured fabric and make a plaid chalk pattern as explained on page 49.

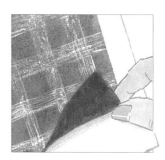

**2** Spray the chalked tissue paper with chalk fixative and leave to dry. Glue the tissue to a piece of stiff white paper.

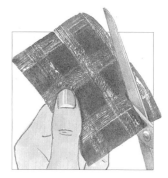

**3** Once the glue is dry, cut the tag to the desired size, making sure that it is large enough to fit your chosen motif (see page 118 for choice of motifs).

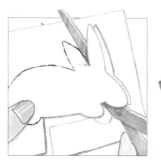

**4** Using the chosen template, cut a motif out of lightweight paper (see page 118 for the bunny shape shown here).

**5** Glue the cutout motif to the center of the chalked plaid tag.

**6** Punch a hole in the end of the tag, and thread a length of grosgrain ribbon through the hole.

## MAKING A CHAIN MOTIF

**1** Using the boy or the girl motif on page 118, make a thin cardboard template.

**2** Cut a long strip of paper as deep as the height of the motif. Using the template, trace the motif onto the end of the strip. (Note that the chain is linked at the hands.)

**3** Fold the strip of paper in accordion pleats so that there are many layers under the traced motif and so that each pleat is the exact width of the motif.

**4** Cut carefully around the top and bottom of the motif through all the layers of paper, but do not cut across the dolls' hands or you will break the chain.

**5** Gently unfold the pleats to reveal the chain of motifs, taking care not to tear the shapes at the folds.

**6** Wrap your gift with chalked paper and secure the chain motif around it with sticky tape.

# CHILD'S BIRTHDAY

Here's a chance to have lots of fun. All children love bright, bold colors and even the youngest enjoys recognizing numbers and letter shapes—especially their own initials.

With the simple cut-paper technique used here children will also enjoy helping paste and decorate presents for family and friends. Choose clear colors and simple shapes to appeal to both boys and girls. Go all out with patterns and papers but keep ties simple. For very small children a gift bag with the present nestling in tissue is a great idea: they can open their own present without the frustration of asking an adult to help.

Don't be downhearted when your carefully wrapped parcel is torn apart—from an under-five it's the greatest compliment!

*The cut-paper motifs featured here are designed especially for a*
*child's birthday. See the following pages for how to decorate*
*a box with cut-paper motifs, and how to make the tags and cards.*
*Directions for making a gift bag (far left) from scratch*
*are given on page 28, and templates for letter and number motifs*
*can be found in the template library on pages 119 and 120.*

# CUT PAPER

This is a fun technique that kids will love. Even small children can participate in this type of paper craft if they are provided with multicolored, precut motifs to stick onto a brightly colored box. Ready-made self-adhesive stickers, so widely available for children, can be added along with the cut ones.

Although the motifs and cut strips are shown here being applied to a spray-painted box, they could be applied randomly to a purchased gift box or to solid-colored wrapping paper before or after the gift is wrapped. As a special touch, try using a novelty punch that cuts shapes such as hearts, stars, or animals (see center tag with dog cutouts in the photograph on page 52).

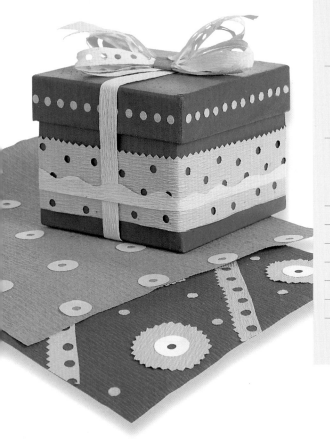

## MATERIALS

### For box

Spray-painted recycled box
or purchased box

### For cut-paper decoration

Selection of brightly colored
papers of medium weight,
such as mock-crepe or
construction paper

Tape measure

Scissors

Pinking shears

Hole punch

Double-sided or sticky tape

Glue

Paper ribbon

## DECORATING A BOX

**1** Spray-paint a box as described on page 26 and allow to dry, or use a purchased gift box. To work out the length required for the decorative bands, measure around the box.

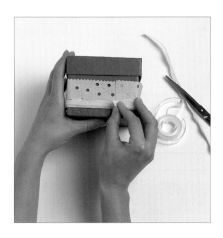

**5** From a contrasting color paper, cut a second strip, narrower than the first strip but the same length. Trim one long edge to form a wavy, irregular line. Wrap this strip around the box over the first strip and secure in the same way.

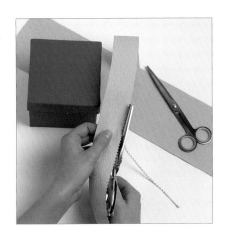

2 Cut a wide strip of paper, long enough to go around the box and overlap at each end by about 1 in (2.5 cm). Using pinking shears, serrate one edge of the strip.

3 Using a hole punch, randomly punch holes all along the strip. Keep the circles of paper created by the hole punch in a little pile to use later for decorating the edge of the lid.

4 Wrap the strip around the base of the box, centering it between the bottom of the box and the lid. Secure in place with tape. Double-sided tape is neatest if you have it.

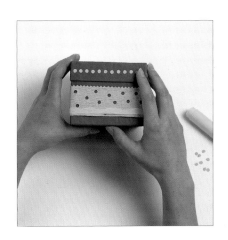

6 Glue the punched hole circles (see Step 3 above) all around the side edges of the box lid, spacing them either uniformly or at random.

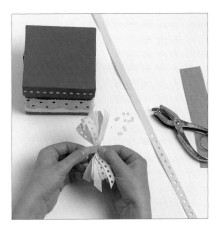

7 Punch holes along the paper ribbon and make a bow in the same way as the raffia bow on page 20. You can make your own paper ribbon from a strip of strong paper.

8 Wrap a length of paper ribbon or a narrow strip of paper around the box and stick the paper bow on top of it using double-sided tape.

# NUMBER AND LETTER TAGS AND CARDS

The best paper to use for these letter and number shapes is a stiff paper that will keep its shape. But if the required color is only available in a light-weight paper, use a stiff white paper for the base and glue the lighter paper on top of it before cutting out the letter or number.

To vary the tags and cards, cut rectangles with scissors or pinking shears for the base, stick on the number or letter, then decorate with ready-made self-adhesive stickers. If you make the base, kids can do the decorating unsupervised.

## MATERIALS

### For templates
Pencil

Tracing paper

Thin card

Scissors

### For number tag
Stiff, brightly colored paper

Scissors

Hole punch

Narrow ribbon

### For letter card
Stiff paper in four bright colors

Scissors

Hole punch

Glue

Pinking shears

Narrow paper ribbon

## MAKING A NUMBER TAG

**1** Make a template using the appropriate number from the template library on page 120. Trace the number onto colored paper, using a pencil.

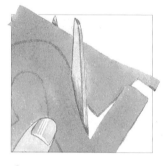

**2** Using straight-edged scissors, cut out the number. To avoid having to erase the pencil outline, cut just inside the pencil line.

**3** Using a hole punch, make holes along the entire length of the number shape making sure the holes are evenly spaced.

**4** Thread a length of narrow ribbon through the topmost hole of the tag.

## MAKING A LETTER CARD

**1** Using one of the letter templates on pages 119 and 120, make a paper letter. Then follow Steps 1–3 for the paper number tag on the previous page.

**2** From a contrasting paper, cut a rectangle slightly larger than your chosen letter. Glue the prepared letter to the center of this rectangle.

**3** Using pinking shears, trim off the contrasting paper, cutting close to the edge of the letter to create a narrow, contrasting pinked border.

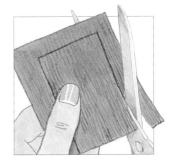

**4** From a third contrasting paper, cut a small rectangle as wide as the letter and about 1 in (2.5 cm) longer.

**5** From a fourth contrasting paper, cut and fold a card backing so that the folded card is at least ¾ in (2 cm) larger all around than the small rectangle cut in Step 4.

**6** Carefully position the small rectangle cut in Step 4 on the front of the folded card to form the background for the hanging letter. Glue in place.

**7** To attach the letter, first use a hole punch to make two holes through the top left of the small rectangle on the card.

**8** Thread a length of narrow paper ribbon through the holes in the card and one hole in the letter, and tie.

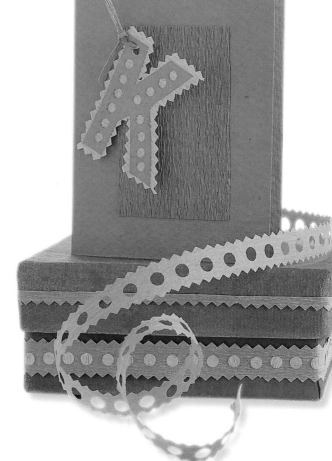

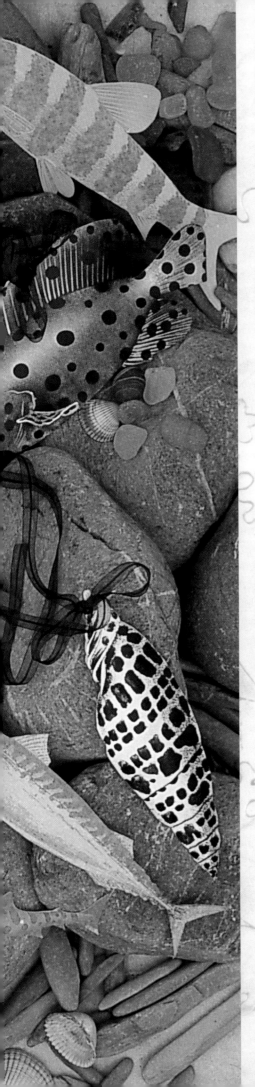

# ADULT BIRTHDAY

A birthday present for a dear friend or member of your family provides you with a great opportunity to demonstrate how much you care. This is a special day, so take time to make your gift wrap unique.

Choose a theme that is personal—perhaps the recipient is interested in golfing or gardening—or you can reflect on a happy time you spent together. Bear in mind the personality of the recipient: outgoing or introvert, practical or romantic. The découpage techniques outlined on the following pages and shown left, can produce sharp and sassy images or soft and muted shapes. Your approach may be sophisticated or simple, but your gift will always be stunning.

*This seaside theme makes a lovely design for presenting a man's or woman's birthday gift. The instructions on the following pages will enable you to make similarly designed découpage boxes, papers, tags, and envelopes using your own choice of motifs. The black and white découpage gift packages with ties are for small presents; they are made the same way as the tree packages on page 93, but with a découpage front and a plain paper back.*

# DECOUPAGE

**For découpage**

Black and white photocopies of
chosen motif or motifs

Scissors

Clear-drying glue

**For box**

Sprayed recycled box

**For gift paper**

Large sheet of medium-weight
tracing paper

Be adventurous when looking for découpage motifs. Choose strong, clear motifs that reflect the recipient's hobbies or interests, but always keep in mind what visual effect the shapes will create. Look for motifs in old magazines and newspapers and photocopy motifs from items you can't cut up. If you are photocopying motifs, remember you can also enlarge or reduce them on many photocopiers. Tracing paper is a very versatile base for découpage, since the motifs can be glued on top of the paper for a bold effect or to the underside for an interesting muted effect. The color of the gift beneath will show through if you use tracing paper for wrapping, so it is best to put the gift in a plain colored box.

## DECORATING A BOX

**1** Spray a recycled box as explained on page 26 and set aside to dry. Photocopy the required number and type of motifs. Cut out the motifs close to their outer edges.

**2** Lay the motifs at equally spaced intervals on the top of the sprayed box. Try different arrangements with the shapes until you have achieved the desired effect.

**3** Glue the cutouts in place. (If you want, you can cover the side of the box in the same way, but arrange the cutouts carefully before gluing them permanently in place.)

## CREATING PAPER WITH A BOLD EFFECT

1 Photocopy your chosen motifs, making sure you have enough to cover your sheet of paper. (Remember that you can enlarge or reduce your motifs on the photocopier if necessary.) Cut out the photocopied motifs close to the outer edges of the shapes.

2 Place the motifs right side up on the right side of the tracing paper and arrange them at regular intervals. Glue the motifs in place.

## ACHIEVING A MUTED EFFECT

1 Photocopy your chosen motifs as for Step 1 above. Then cut out the photocopied motifs close to the outer edges of the shapes.

2 Place the motifs face down on the wrong side of the tracing paper, arranging them at regular intervals. Spread glue over the right side of each motif and stick it in place.

61

# DECOUPAGE TAGS AND ENVELOPES

Découpage cutouts can be arranged at regular intervals as shown on the gift paper and the box on the previous pages or, alternatively, placed at random or even overlapping. They can also be used individually as shown here for the tags.

To introduce color into your découpage designs, add brightly colored tissue to your photocopied black and white motifs or use colored cutouts from magazines and newspapers. Photocopying motifs onto colored paper is another interesting design possibility to try.

## MATERIALS

### For découpage

Black and white photocopies of the chosen motif or motifs

Scissors

Clear-drying glue

### For decoration

Scraps of brightly colored tissue paper in assorted colors

### For envelope

Medium-weight tracing paper

### For tags

Large sheet of medium-weight tracing paper

Hole punch

Narrow ribbon

## MAKING A DÉCOUPAGE ENVELOPE

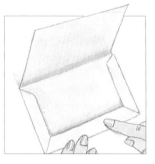

1 Using the template for the envelope with flaps on page 113, transfer the envelope shape onto a piece of medium-weight tracing paper, and cut out.

2 Score the fold lines as explained on page 25. Crease the fold lines carefully, then fold the envelope together. Unfold the envelope and set aside.

3 Make photocopies of your chosen motif or motifs, enlarging if necessary, and cut them out close to the outer edges of the shapes.

4 Apply glue to the right side of each motif and glue right side down to the wrong side of the front of the envelope.

5 As the contents will show through, make a matching card. Cut an oblong of tracing paper which will fit inside the envelope.

6 Decorate the paper with torn strips of tissue. Refold the envelope and glue the flaps in place before slipping the card inside.

## MAKING A TISSUE-COVERED TAG

**1** Make a photocopy of your chosen motif. Apply glue to the right side of the motif, and press on a scrap of colored tissue paper.

**2** Once the glue has dried thoroughly, cut out the tag. Keep close to the outer edge of the motif and cut through both layers.

**3** For a decorative effect, place the motif under the ribbon on your present. Or, to make it into a tag, punch a hole and add a ribbon tie.

## MAKING A TORN-TISSUE TAG

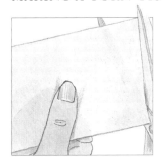   

**1** Make a photocopy of your chosen motif. Cut a piece of tracing paper that is about ½ in (12 mm) larger all around than the motif.

**2** Tear random strips of tissue paper in a few contrasting colors. Arrange these strips on the tracing paper tag, and glue in place.

**3** Cut out the découpage motif, and glue it, right side up, to the center of the tag on top of the torn tissue.

**4** Using a hole punch, punch a hole in the corner of the tag, and thread a length of narrow ribbon through the hole.

# VALENTINE'S DAY

What better way to show your Valentine that you really care than to spend a little time decorating and wrapping your gifts in a special way with handmade papers, cards, and tags.

The tradition of lovers exchanging gifts and cards on February 14th can be traced back to the Roman fertility festival, Lupercalia, which was held on February 15th. It is really an accident of history that Saint Valentine's feast day became connected with the tradition. Valentine's Day as we know it was first celebrated in the seventeenth century, when gentlemen sent ladies Valentine's Day gifts and handmade cards. These were often decorated with hearts and flowers—a custom that continues today.

In the gifts pictured here, a rich blend of browns and deep reds, combined with glittering gold, gives a new, stylish look to the traditional Valentine colors of bright red and gold.

*The techniques for stenciling on gift paper and for making paper roses are shown on the following pages. An assortment of alternative heart shapes for stenciling can be found in the template directory on page 121. See page 22 for how to make the embellished bow (top right) and page 21 for the bow with trailers (top left).*

# STENCILING

Stenciling is a fast and stylish way to decorate wrapping paper. Forget the time-consuming techniques needed for stenciling on walls or furniture: work quickly, holding the stencil in place with one hand and dabbing the paintbrush with the other. The lucky recipient of the gift is not going to notice the occasional mis-aligned motif when the overall effect is so stunning. Stenciled hearts are the perfect decoration for a Valentine's Day gift, but for a less traditional theme you can select flower motifs (see page 121) or choose a motif that means something special to your Valentine. The tags here and on pages 64 and 65 are stenciled, with relief-paint details applied as highlights.

## MATERIALS

### For stenciling
Pencil

Tracing paper

Stiff scrap paper for stencil

Utility knife

Cutting mat

Gold and red poster paint

Soft stencil brush

Old newspapers or other scrap paper for protecting work surface

### For gift paper
Plain or marbled paper

### For tag
Scraps of contrasting colored or marbled paper

Scissors

Glue stick

Hole punch

Gold plastic relief paint

Ribbon

## DECORATING GIFT PAPER

**1** To make a stencil for the large heart, trace the large heart shape (see page 121) onto tracing paper using a pencil, then transfer it to stiff paper. Cut out the shape using a utility knife and a cutting mat. Trim the border of the stencil to about ¾ in (2 cm) around the heart.

## MAKING A TAG

**1** Following the steps above for the stenciling technique, stencil a large heart onto a scrap of colored or marbled paper (see page 121 for heart templates in various sizes). Cut the shape out, leaving a border of unpainted background paper around the edge of the heart about ¼ in (6 mm) wide.

2 Place the gift paper on a surface protected with old newspapers or other scrap paper. Hold the stencil in place on the paper, and holding the nearly dry brush upright, stipple the paint into the heart shape.

3 Continue painting hearts at random on the paper in the same way, being careful not to overlap the stencil border onto the wet hearts. When there are enough large hearts to cover the paper (with generous spaces in between), leave the paint to dry for a few minutes before going on to the next step.

4 Make a stencil for the small heart following the instructions for the large heart (see Step 1 left). Stencil the small hearts onto the paper in the spaces between the large hearts. Allow to dry completely before using the paper to wrap your gift.

2 From a piece of contrasting paper, cut a rectangle larger than the cut-out heart. Then, using a glue stick, glue the cut-out heart to the center of the contrasting paper.

3 You can either leave the tag rectangular or again cut around the heart about ¼ in (6 mm) from the edge of the first heart to form a second contrasting border. At this stage you can turn your tag into a card by sticking it onto a folded piece of plain or colored stiff paper.

4 For the tag, punch a hole at the top of the heart and thread a length of narrow ribbon through the hole. Using gold plastic relief paint, apply a line of dots around the stenciled heart; then carefully draw a small heart in the center of the tag.

# PAPER ROSES

Flowers provide a charming finishing touch to gifts of all shapes and sizes. Used to embellish an envelope, they can even transform a simple card into a keepsake. Sophisticated paper flowers are surprisingly easy to make and a posy can be completed in just a matter of minutes. The roses shown here are made from crepe paper and from a medium-weight marbled paper, but other types of paper give equally good results. Match the colors to your gift wrapping paper and experiment with different papers.

## MATERIALS

**For transferring templates**

Pencil

Tracing paper

**For paper rose**

Lightweight paper

Scissors

Dull kitchen knife

Glue

Gold paint and brush (optional)

**For paper leaves**

Lightweight gold paper

Scissors

Pinking shears (optional)

Narrow satin ribbon

**For posy of roses**

Paper rose and rosebud

Three paper leaves

Glue

Narrow satin ribbon or tissue paper

## MAKING A ROSE

1 Using the rose template on page 122, cut the rose shape from your chosen paper.

2 Using a dull knife and your thumb, curl the top edges of the outer petals outward as shown.

3 Beginning at the "C" end of the flower shape, roll up the paper tightly for a few turns to form the center of the rose.

4 Rolling the rest of the rose loosely, dot the "stem" points with glue as you go, and squeeze and twist them together to secure.

5 When the rose is completely rolled, use a dot of glue to secure the final petal edge in place.

6 If you wish, you can highlight the top of the rose with a few brush strokes of gold paint.

## MAKING A ROSE LEAF FOR A SINGLE ROSE

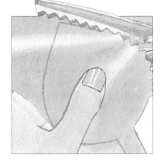  

**1** Using the template on page 122, cut out the leaf from your chosen paper. If you are in a hurry, cut the edge with pinking shears.

**2** Fold the cut-out leaf in half lengthwise to crease the center and create a veined effect.

**3** Unfold the leaf, glue it to the base of the rose, then tie with a length of narrow satin ribbon.

## MAKING A ROSE POSY

**1** Make a rosebud exactly as for the rose on the left, but using the rosebud template on page 122. Then make a full-blown rose using the same paper.

**2** Using the leaf templates on page 122 and your choice of paper for the leaves, make two or three leaves as explained above.

**3** Glue the leaves, rosebud, and rose together, then tie with ribbon or wrap with a strip of tissue paper secured with glue.

# EASTER

Easter heralds a time of new growth and rebirth. For children it means the Easter bunny, egg hunts, chicks, and chocolate—lots of it. For adults Easter is often a time of renewal and contemplation, when a thoughtful gift from a loved one will be received with joy.

Here golden yellow, cool leafy green, clear sky blue, and accents of ice white are used to create a fresh palette with which to decorate Easter gifts. With a simple-to-do but very unusual technique—bleaching—fine tissue paper is patterned with flowers, stars, circles, and squares. Use this decorated paper to give wrapped chocolate eggs a distinctive touch. Paper flowers replace traditional ribbons and bows, and also decorate cards. Flower tags add the finishing touch.

*Brightly colored tissue paper with bleached patterns sets the scene for these striking Easter presents. The step-by-step instructions for making the bleached paper and for using it to wrap Easter eggs are given on the next two pages. See pages 74 and 75 for how to make the flowers, cards, and tags, and page 123 for a choice of three-dimensional flower templates.*

# BLEACHED PAPER

Tissue is the best paper to use for bleached patterns. Needing only a weak solution of bleach, tissue loses its color easily and dries quickly. Although bleaching patterns into paper is a simple technique, requiring no drawing skill, it is still not a suitable craft for young children and you must make sure bleach is kept well out of their reach. The best patterns for bleaching are those that can be worked quickly, such as dots, circles, crosses, triangles, checks, or simple flowers. If more complicated shapes are preferred, a template and pencil can be used to transfer motifs to the tissue before the outlines are painted on.

## MATERIALS

### For bleaching

Sheet of plastic and a large sheet of white scrap paper for protecting the work surface

Liquid bleach

Container for water and bleach solution

Paintbrush

### For gift paper

Brightly colored tissue paper

### For wrapping chocolate egg

Tissue paper 8 x 10 in
(20 x 25 cm)

Foil-wrapped chocolate egg about the size of a hen's egg

Small paper flower, leaf and stem templates on page 123

Scissors

Paper ribbon

## MAKING BLEACHED TISSUE PAPER

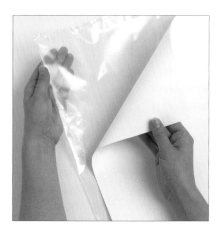

**1** Cover your work surface with a sheet of plastic and a large sheet of white scrap paper. Make sure that the plastic sheet has no holes in it and, even when taking these precautions, do not use this technique near valuable items of furniture. Always keep bleach out of the reach of small children.

## TISSUE WRAPPING A CHOCOLATE EGG

**1** Cut a 8 x 10 in (20 x 25 cm) rectangle of tissue paper, then decorate it with dots or another simple pattern, following the bleaching instructions given above. Let the paper dry before continuing.

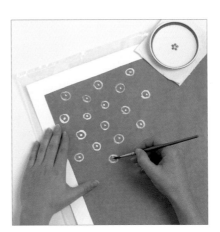

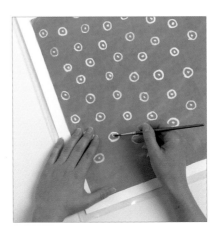

2 Fill a container with water and add a little liquid bleach. Using a paintbrush, test the strength of the solution on a scrap of tissue paper. The color should come out right away. If it does not, add a little more bleach to the water and test again on another scrap of tissue.

3 Dip the paintbrush in the solution and mark your chosen tissue paper with a simple design such as crosses, checks, spots, circles, or flowers, placing the motifs at random. Be careful not to overload the brush with the bleach solution or your design will bleed.

4 Continue covering the tissue paper with motifs until you are happy with the result. When working, do not worry about small splatters of bleach, as these will add to the attractive handmade quality of the paper. Let the paper dry completely before wrapping your gift.

2 Wrap the foil-covered chocolate egg with the decorated tissue paper, gathering the paper together at the top of the egg.

3 Wrap a length of paper ribbon carefully around the gathered tissue and tie it into a bow, leaving long loose ends. Then curl each end of the ribbon by drawing it carefully between your thumb and a scissor blade.

4 Make a small paper flower with a long stem and leaf (see page 74 for instructions, and page 123 for templates). Insert the stem of the paper flower under the paper ribbon behind the bow.

# PAPER FLOWERS

These three-dimensional paper flowers are made by cutting flat flower layers and joining them at the center to a twisted paper stem. The templates for the petals and leaves are on page 123.

The paper flowers can be tucked under a bow to decorate a gift, stuck to a piece of contrasting paper to form a tag or card, or the individual flat flower shapes can simply be strung on a length of knotted paper ribbon to make a pretty flower chain. Follow the color scheme shown here or create your own.

## MATERIALS

**For flower templates**

Pencil

Tracing paper

Stiff scrap paper

Scissors

**For paper flowers**

Stiff, medium-weight paper in yellow, white, orange, and green

Scissors

Glue

Craft stiletto or large needle (for piercing holes)

**For tag or card**

Stiff, medium-weight paper in yellow, white, green, and turquoise

Scissors

Glue

Craft stiletto (for piercing holes)

Hole punch

Paper ribbon

MAKING A PAPER FLOWER

**1** Using the templates on page 123, transfer the two outer flower petal shapes onto yellow or other base color paper and cut them both out.

**2** Transfer the central scalloped flower petal shape onto white paper and the circular flower center onto orange paper, then cut them both out.

**3** Transfer the stem template onto green paper and cut out. Roll the stem paper to form a long, thin stem shape with one end tapering to a point.

**4** Lay the orange center on top of the white scalloped petal, then lay these two on top of the yellow outer petals.

**5** Holding all four layers together securely, pierce a hole through the center of all the layers, using a craft stiletto or a large needle.

**6** Push the tapered tip of the stem through the holes from the front of the flower layers to the back. Dot with glue to secure if necessary.

## MAKING A DAISY TAG OR CARD

**1** Using the templates on page 123, transfer the stem onto turquoise paper, the three daisy petal shapes onto white paper, and a flower center onto yellow paper. Make up as for the flower shown left.

**2** Using the templates on page 123, cut two large leaves from green paper. Then fold each leaf in half lengthwise to crease the center.

**3** Unfold the leaves and pierce a hole through the end of each. Add them to the daisy by pushing the tapered tip of the stem through the holes and securing with a dab of glue.

**4** Clip off the end of the stem close to the wrong side of the flower.

**5** Using the template on page 123, cut the tag base from yellow paper, and glue the paper daisy and leaves to the center of this shape.

**6** To complete the tag, punch a hole in one of the corners of the yellow-paper base and thread a length of narrow paper ribbon through the hole.

**7** Make a folded white card 7 in (18 cm) square. Cut a 3½ in (9 cm) square of turquoise paper and glue it to the center of the card.

**8** Finally, glue the finished tag to the center of the turquoise square, placing it at a slight angle.

# MOTHER'S DAY

Traditionally mothers receive a bouquet of flowers on Mother's Day. More recently, however, a popular trend is to give longer-lasting presents, such as a potted plant, a scarf, or even a small piece of jewelry. Such special gifts give her added pleasure and help you say "thank you."

Of all people, mothers especially appreciate gifts and wrappings that are handmade by their children. Here crepe paper in soft, muted colors has been used to wrap, decorate, make gift tags, and even to tie parcels. Children will enjoy rolling paper into lengths of string and they will love the artistry of using torn colored paper and glue to make decorated paper and tags. Adults can help make ruffled paper bags to contain awkwardly shaped presents or a precious homemade gift.

*The theme for these Mother's Day gifts is torn-paper decorations, and all the wrappings shown here—from the gift paper to the tags, ruffles, and paper string—are made from crepe paper. Instructions for decorating the tags and gift paper are given on the following pages. The simple finishing touches—crepe paper bags with paper ruffles and handmade paper string—are explained on pages 80 and 81. Turn to page 16 for directions for wrapping a round box (far left).*

# TORN PAPER

Torn-paper decoration is a quick and easy gift wrapping technique. All that is needed is an assortment of contrasting colored paper and a glue stick. Note that liquid glue or types of glue other than a glue stick may affect the color of the crepe paper. If you don't have time to decorate a whole sheet of paper with the roughly torn shapes, just decorate a band to wrap around the center of a gift that has already been wrapped with a plain paper in a contrasting color.

Although torn-paper decorations can be made with any soft paper that tears easily, crepe paper is especially suited to this technique. As crepe paper is very malleable and can be stretched, the shapes can be glued flat to the base paper, or crumpled up or stretched to create three-dimensional effects. Large torn strips of paper can even be flared out to form asymmetrical ruffle shapes. How to form crepe-paper ruffles is explained on page 81.

## MATERIALS

### For gift paper

| |
|---|
| Crepe paper in a few contrasting colors |
| Scrap of thin cardboard for flower template |
| Pencil |
| Scissors |
| Glue stick |

### For tag

| |
|---|
| Piece of stiff paper for tag base |
| Crepe paper in a few contrasting colors |
| Scissors |
| Glue stick |
| Hole punch |
| Paper string (see page 80) |

## DECORATING WITH TORN PAPER

**1** Using the scalloped flower templates on page 123 and a pencil, draw the shapes on crepe paper. Then, pressing the paper between the thumb and index finger of one hand and tearing with the other hand, tear out the flower shapes as close as possible to the pencil line. The torn shapes do not have to be precise.

## MAKING A TORN-PAPER TAG

**1** Using a glue stick, glue a piece of crepe paper to a piece of stiff paper. Then cut out the tag to the required size and shape.

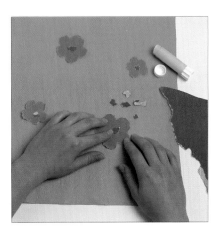

2 Always use a glue stick instead of liquid glue with crepe paper, as liquid glue can sometimes discolor crepe paper. Rub the glue stick over the wrong side of a torn-paper flower. Then glue the flower to your chosen gift paper. Glue the remaining flower shapes at random to the gift paper, leaving spaces in between.

3 Take a piece of crepe paper in a contrasting color to the flowers. Tear tiny pieces from it. Then, using the glue stick, glue one piece to the center of each flower.

4 Tear small specks and short thin strips from other contrasting crepe papers. Use these odd shapes to fill in the spaces between the torn-paper flowers. If you are using "double-sided" crepe papers that have a different color on each side, allow some of the strips to curl outward to reveal the color underneath.

2 Tear random strips from a contrasting crepe paper and glue them to the tag to make a pattern. Don't worry about tearing straight lines or exact shapes.

3 Using another contrasting color, tear out small pieces and arrange them on the tag. Glue these torn shapes in place to complete the abstract design, then trim the ends of the strips that overlap the edge of the tag.

4 Punch a hole in a corner of the tag and thread a length of thin paper string through the hole. See page 80 for how to make the paper string from strips of crepe paper.

## CREPE-PAPER BAGS

A crepe-paper bag is a perfect container for a small gift or for a few wrapped chocolates. Crepe paper is stretchy, yet strong, and so the best paper for this type of bag. Look out for double-sided crepe paper, with a different color on each side. Other soft, flexible papers such as tissue paper or cellophane, can also be used.

The ruffle on the bag is made in one long strip tied in place with homemade crepe-paper string. The asymmetrical torn-paper ruffles on the tags on page 76 are rolled, stretched, and flared into shape in exactly the same way as the bag ruffle.

### MATERIALS

**For crepe-paper bag**

Crepe paper in at least three contrasting shades

Scissors

Glue stick

**For paper string**

Long strip of crepe paper

Scissors

### MAKING PAPER STRING

1 Cut a strip of crepe paper across the grain of the paper. For a wide string, cut the strip about 3 in (8 cm) wide; for a thin string, about ½ in (12 mm) wide.

2 Beginning at one end of the strip, roll it diagonally between the tips of your fingers, twisting it as you go.

3 Continue twisting the strip of crepe paper until the paper string is the required length.

4 Using a pair of scissors, trim the ends of the string to neaten them. Make a few lengths of string in this way to keep for future use.

## MAKING A BAG WITH A PAPER RUFFLE

**1** Cut out a 16 x 14 in (40 cm x 35 cm) piece of crepe paper, with the longer edge running with the grain of the paper.

**2** Fold the piece of crepe paper in half across the grain of the paper.

**3** Glue the two layers of the folded bag together along the short sides, using a glue stick.

**4** Gather the bag together and roll it gently between the palms of your hands to create wrinkles that follow the grain of the paper. Set the bag aside.

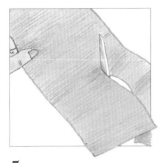

**5** From a contrasting crepe paper, cut a 10 x 5½ in (25 x 14 cm) strip for the ruffle, with the short edge running with the grain. Roll the strip as in Step 4.

**6** Smooth out the bag and ruffle without flattening the creases. Then decorate the bag or the ruffle with small pieces of torn paper.

**7** Fill the bag with a small gift, then wrap the ruffle around the neck of the bag and secure it with a length of paper string (facing page).

**8** Gently pulling the crepe with your fingertips, stretch out the top and bottom edges of the crepe paper ruffle to flare them.

**9** Flare out the top edge of the crepe bag in the same way to complete the decorative effect.

# FATHER'S DAY

Father's Day gives everyone, whether grown-up or child, the opportunity to spoil their dad with treats and special gifts. And every father will enjoy being the center of attention with skillfully wrapped presents chosen specially to surprise and please.

There's a bit of the country-lover in almost every man, which is why these wrappings with a rural theme have been chosen. Using rubber stamps and textured card and paper, the look is rugged and masculine. Strong rustic colors, including browns and greens, enhance the masculine effect. Children young and old enjoy decorating paper, tags, and cards with ready-made rubber stamps. For a spontaneous effect, you can create your own unique stamping tools using cut fruit and vegetables.

*Rubber stamps can be purchased in a wide range of motifs, from letters and numbers to flowers and animals. The bees, butterflies, and hedgehogs used here provide a suitable theme for Father's Day. Stamping techniques for gift paper, cards, and tags are explained on the following pages. If you want to make a corrugated flatpack for your gift (upper left-hand corner) or pleated-paper stuffing, see pages 27 and 87 respectively.*

## MATERIALS

### For rubber stamping

Rubber stamp or stamps

One or two colors of ink pad

### For gift paper or band

Light- or medium-weight
paper with a fairly
smooth surface

### For vegetable stamping

Large carrot or small potato

Sharp knife and cutting board
for cutting vegetable

Rubber stamp

Two ink pads, one in a
bright color and one in
a dark color

# STAMPED PAPER

When making stamped paper, you can personalize the gift by choosing a stamp that echoes the recipient's pastimes, interests, or dreams, or by using rubber-stamp letters for initials.

Any type of paper can be used for rubber stamping as long as it is neither too highly textured nor too glossy to take the stamp imprint. It is usually best to stamp a bright or light paper with a darker ink to accentuate the fine lines of the stamp motif. You should always test the stamp and the ink on a scrap of your chosen paper before starting the project.

You can also use a homemade stamp as a contrasting backdrop for the rubber-stamp motif or on its own. Try stamps cut from fruit and vegetables, such as oranges, potatoes, and carrots.

MAKING GIFT PAPER

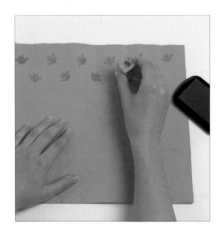

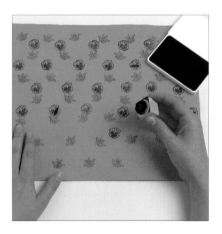

**1** First press the rubber stamp onto the ink pad, then press the inked stamp onto a scrap of your chosen paper to check results. Now lay your gift paper on a flat, hard surface and smooth it out. Stamp, arranging the pattern at random or in rows, reapplying the ink after each impression.

**2** Continue stamping the paper until the whole piece is covered. Let the ink dry thoroughly before using the paper to wrap your present.

**3** For an alternative design, stamp the paper as for Steps 1 and 2, then fill in the spaces between the first stamped motifs with another, complementary stamp design, using a contrasting colored ink.

## MAKING A GIFT BAND

**1** For a stamped band to wrap around a present, first cut a strip of paper about 1 in (2.5 cm) wider than the stamp, and long enough to fit around your present and overlap at the ends by about 1½ in (4 cm).

**2** Stamp motifs all along the center of the strip at equally spaced intervals. Allow the ink to dry before wrapping the band around a colored box or a wrapped gift.

## MAKING A VEGETABLE-STAMP PATTERN

**1** Cut off the top of a small potato, making sure that the surface is as flat as possible. For other stamp shapes, you could also try using cut carrots, oranges, or lemons.

**2** Press the flat surface of the potato firmly onto the ink pad, then onto the gift paper. Cover the paper at random or in even or staggered rows with the circular shapes. Let the ink dry for a few minutes.

**3** You may be happy with your design as it stands, but if you wish, you can use a darker ink and a rubber stamp to apply a motif in the center of each potato-stamped circle to complete the effect.

# STAMPED TAGS AND CARDS

As stamped motifs need to be applied to smooth papers they create flat images, so look especially attractive when juxtaposed with various contrasting textured surfaces. Stamped designs cut out and combined with corrugated paper, plastic relief paint, and string make highly effective tags and cards. Self-adhesive foam mounts, available from craft stores, create great three-dimensional effects.

Brown pleated-paper stuffing spilling out of a gift box decorated with stamps completes these textured compositions wonderfully.

## MATERIALS

**For stamping**

Rubber stamp of your choice

Ink pad

**For tag**

Stiff medium-weight paper in three contrasting colors

Scissors

Glue

Hole punch

Self-adhesive hole reinforcement

Colored fine string

**For three-dimensional card**

Corrugated paper in two contrasting colors

Stiff, medium-weight paper in two contrasting colors

Self-adhesive foam mounts

Scissors

Glue

Plastic relief paint

**For pleated-paper stuffing**

Lightweight brown paper

Scissors

## MAKING A GIFT TAG

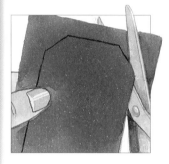

**1** Cut a "luggage" tag shape of your preferred size from a piece of medium-weight paper, using one of the templates on page 115.

**2** Stamp two motifs onto a small piece of contrasting paper and then three onto another small piece of contrasting paper.

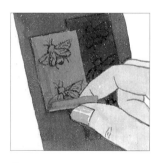

**3** Trim the two stamped papers close to the motifs, then glue them to the tag so that they overlap.

**4** Punch a hole at the top of the tag, stick on a hole reinforcement, and tie on a length of fine string.

## MAKING A THREE-DIMENSIONAL CARD

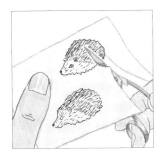

**1** Stamp your chosen motif twice onto a piece of colored paper and cut out each of the two shapes close to their outlines.

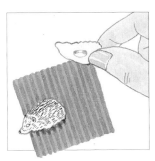

**2** Cut out a square of corrugated paper big enough for the two motifs. Stick the motifs to the square with foam mounts.

**3** Cut a larger square of paper in another contrasting color, and glue the corrugated square with the stamped motifs on top of it.

**4** Cut a piece of corrugated paper and fold it in half to make the base, ensuring it is ¾ in (2 cm) larger all around than the decorated square.

**5** Then glue the stamped decoration to the center of the front of the corrugated card base.

**6** Decorate the edge of the inner border of the finished card with dots of plastic relief paint.

## MAKING PLEATED-PAPER STUFFING

**1** Cut a long strip of lightweight brown paper. Fold over a narrow pleat at one end of the strip. Continue pleating the paper widthwise, as finely as possible, in accordion fashion as shown above. Try to keep the pleats square to the edge of the paper.

**2** Holding the pleats in place between your thumb and forefinger, cut the brown paper into very narrow strips. Let the strips unravel to form long pieces of creased stuffing. Use the pieces to fill and pad out a gift bag or box decorated with stamps.

# TRADITIONAL CHRISTMAS

The festive season provides a wonderful opportunity to brighten your home with beautifully wrapped presents and eye-catching greeting cards in cheerful traditional colors.

Here the Christmas theme is unified with subtle dry-brush stenciling on traditional red and gold. Boxes are sprayed with gold and overlaid with soft white to make a package that is a gift in itself. Traditional tags shaped as holly or ivy give an accent note in green. Finishing touches from nature such as pine cones and acorns will make your gifts truly seasonal.

Tiny gifts including jewelry and fine candy can be packaged as angels, holly, or little Christmas trees, and either hung on the tree or placed on the table as decorative presents.

*Dry-brush stenciling over traditional colors gives a fresh look to these Christmas designs. Full instructions for stenciling motifs on spray-painted boxes and for making shaped tags and the Christmas-tree-, star-, angel-, and holly-shaped packages, are given on the following pages.*

89

# DRY-BRUSH STENCILING

Dry-brush stenciling generally looks best when applied to large motifs with bold rather than intricate shapes. The secret to successful dry-brush stenciling is to mix the paint to a thick consistency and apply it sparingly. When the paint is brushed over the stencil, the bristles of the brush will separate giving an interesting, streaked effect. The paint will dry in seconds. The templates on pages 124 and 125 provide designs suitable for this bold decorative technique.

Dry-brush stenciling can be worked onto gift paper, but it is shown here worked directly onto spray-painted boxes. When you package your gift in a hand-stenciled box, the box itself becomes a much valued part of the gift, so it is well worth making that extra effort to finish the box carefully.

## MATERIALS

### For stencil templates
Pencil

Tracing paper

Scrap paper for stencil

Utility knife

Cutting mat

### For box
Red, green, or gold spray paint

New or recycled box with lid

Old newspapers or other scrap paper for protecting the work surface

### For star decorations
Tube of gold acrylic paint

Dry, stiff flat-ended brush

### For stripe decorations
Masking tape

Tubes of silver and white acrylic paints

Dry, stiff flat-ended brush

## DECORATING WITH STARS

1 Cover your work surface with old newspapers or scrap paper. Spray an old box following the instructions on page 26 or use a purchased gift box. While the box is drying, test your brush and paint on a piece of scrap paper to ensure that the brush strokes provide the desired effect.

## DECORATING WITH STRIPES

1 Using gold spray paint, cover the box and lid as in Step 1 of decorating with stars above. When the spray paint is completely dry, put the lid on the box. Then wrap evenly spaced lines of masking tape around the closed box.

2 Using the templates on page 124, cut a stencil for the large star as described in Step 1 for stenciling gift paper on page 66. Position the large star stencil on the box. Dab the brush lightly into the gold paint, then brush quickly over the star stencil, working in different directions.

3 Cover both the lid and the box with widely spaced, large stenciled stars. At the box edges bend the stencil over the edge to continue the shape along the adjacent side. Allow the paint to dry.

4 Cut a stencil for the small star in the same way as you did for the large star. Stencil small stars to fill in the spaces between the large stars.

2 Test the paint and paintbrush as in Step 1 above, then apply strokes of silver paint on the box in between the masking tape, brushing in different directions. Leave the bottom of the box and the ends of the box without masking tape unpainted. Allow the paint to dry.

3 Highlight the silver stripes with a few random strokes of white paint to add to the textured effect of the dry brush stokes.

4 When the paint is dry, remove the masking tape. This simple striped technique can also be used to decorate gift paper.

# SHAPED TAGS AND TREE PACKAGES

## MATERIALS

### For templates
Pencil

Tracing paper

Scrap of stiff paper

Scissors

### For shaped tag
Stiff green, red, or gold paper

Tube of gold or silver acrylic paint

Glitter glue (optional)

Dry stiff, flat-ended brush

Scissors

Hole punch

Fine gold string or embroidery thread

### For tree package
Stiff green, red, gold, or white paper

Tubes of gold, bronze, silver, and white acrylic paint

Dry stiff, flat-ended brush

Scissors

Strong glue

Hole punch

Fine gold string or embroidery thread

Shaped tags provide a great ornamental finishing touch for a Christmas present.

Tree-shaped gift packages are made in much the same way as the tags but are formed with two layers instead of one. Holly-, ornament-, and angel-shaped tags and packages can be made in the same way using the templates on page 125. These decorative tags and packages can be hung on the tree as ornaments before the big day.

## MAKING A STAR-SHAPED TAG

1 Using the large star template from page 124, transfer the shape onto red, green, or gold paper. Then, using a stiff brush, make random dry brush strokes.

2 Allow the paint to dry. If the paint has obscured the outline, retrace the template shape onto the painted paper. Then cut out the tag.

3 If you wish, you can highlight the painted shape with glitter glue and smear the glue with your fingertip to soften the effect.

4 Punch a hole in the end of the tag, and thread a length of fine gold string or embroidery thread through the hole.

## MAKING A TREE-SHAPED PACKAGE

**1** Using the Christmas tree template from page 124, trace the shape twice onto colored paper.

**2** Trace the tree star from page 124 separately onto gold paper.

**3** Using acrylic paint and a stiff brush, decorate the tree shape, applying the paint sparingly to form dry brush strokes.

**4** Using a second color of paint, apply a few more brush strokes to create highlights.

**5** Decorate the tree star in the same way, using one or two colors of paint as desired.

**6** Let the paint dry completely, then cut out both package shapes.

**7** Glue the star to the top of the front piece of the tree-shaped package. Let the glue dry thoroughly.

**8** Glue the two layers of the package together, leaving the top open for inserting a gift. Let the glue dry thoroughly.

**9** Punch a hole in the top of the star, and thread a length of fine gold string or embroidery thread through the hole.

# COUNTRY CHRISTMAS

Carol singing, long walks in the countryside, church bells, stockings hung around an open hearth—these are the things that spell a perfect Christmas. Gifts of homemade preserves with simple fabric covers, cheery stockings crammed to bursting with small presents—both children and adults will delight in receiving a selection of thoughtful gifts chosen with just them in mind.

Use bright fabrics in cheerful contrasting colors to fashion tags and cards. The look is easy on the eye and easy to create with small remnants of material. Make bags to wrap awkwardly shaped presents and decorate them with simple motifs. With a minimum of sewing expertise you can put together a delightful Christmas stocking for each house guest—a reminder of a perfect Christmas that can be used year after year.

*All the Christmas designs here are decorated with raw-edged fabric shapes attached with fabric glue. Only the bag and stocking require simple running-stitch seams. Turn to the following pages for the steps showing how to make the stocking. The stocking instructions are followed by detailed explanations of how to make the tags, cards, and a present bag. Use fabric remnants for wrapping presents and for cutting strips for ribbons (center left).*

# FABRIC-COLLAGE STOCKING

Stockings filled with tiny presents are one of the enduring child-hood memories of Christmas. Stockings are kept from year to year and even adults will hang them out in the expectation of finding them filled with goodies on Christmas morning! This stocking is decorated with glued-on motifs and small buttons. Although hearts have been used here, you can choose any of the Christmas motifs in the template library. Those shown on the left-hand side of the page will provide additional inspiration.

Making the stocking involves a minimum of sewing, as only the outer edges of the stocking are stitched. The instructions call for a simple running stitch, but if you have a sewing machine, you could use a straight machine stitch instead.

## MATERIALS

### For stocking

Red-and-white plaid for stocking pieces, 24 x 20 in (60 x 50 cm)

Blue-and-white plaid for top band, 4½ x 14 in (12 x 36 cm)

Dressmaking pins

Strong white sewing thread and sewing needle

Scissors and fabric glue

### For fabric collage

Scraps of red-and-white check fabric and calico

Fabric glue

6 small, flat cream buttons

Thick red thread and large needle for attaching buttons

### For templates and paper patterns

Tracing paper and stiff paper for motif templates

Lightweight paper for stocking patterns

Pencil

## MAKING A STOCKING

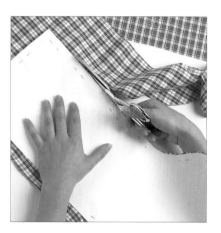

**1** Cut a stocking band piece 4½ x 14 in (12 x 36 cm) from the blue-and-white plaid. Then, using the template on page 126, make a paper pattern piece for the stocking, and use this to cut out two stocking pieces from the red-and-white plaid.

**5** With the wrong sides facing, pin the folded edges of the front and back pieces of the stocking together. Stitch the stocking pieces together close to the edge, working a short, even running stitch and using a sewing needle and strong white sewing thread.

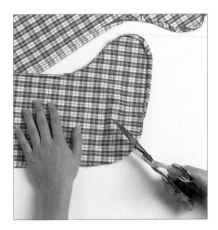

2 Make templates from the small and large hearts on page 126 and use these to cut a small heart from the red-and-white check and a large one from calico. Using fabric glue, glue the small red heart to the large calico heart, then glue them to the front stocking piece 6 in (15 cm) below the top edge.

3 Using thick red thread, attach a button to the center of the top of the calico heart, securing it in place with a knot. Clip the thread ends about ¼ in (6 mm) from the button. Make a small bow with the thick red thread and glue it to the small red-and-white check heart.

4 Clip the seam allowance along the curves as necessary for the fabric to lie flat. Fold under the raw edges of the fabric, pressing ½ in (12 mm) to the wrong side along the raw edge of each stocking piece, omitting the top edge.

6 Press ½ in (12 mm) to the wrong side along the long top edge of the blue-and-white plaid band, then pin the band to the top of the stocking, placing the folded edge over the raw edge of the stocking. (The band should hide the raw edge.) The overlap should be at the back of the stocking. Glue the overlap in place.

7 Stitch the band in place close to the top edge of the stocking, working a short, even running stitch and using strong white sewing thread.

8 Using thick red thread and securing with a knot on the right side as you did the button on the heart, attach six equally spaced buttons along the lower edge of the blue-and-white plaid on the front of the stocking. If desired, stitch a fabric or ribbon loop to the top edge of the stocking at the back seam.

# FABRIC-COLLAGE CARDS AND BAGS

## MATERIALS

### For card

Stiff white paper, 6½ x 13 in (16 x 32 cm) for card backing

Scraps of fabric in red-and-white check, red-and-white plaid, and calico

Scissors

Fabric glue

4 small, flat cream buttons

Thick green thread and large needle

### For present bag

Blue-and-white plaid for bag, 15 x 39½ in (38 x 100 cm)

Calico for pocket 8½ x 9 in (22 x 23 cm), and two pieces for casings 3 x 15½ in (7 x 40 cm)

Red and white plaid for drawstring, 1 x 42 in (2.5 x 106 cm)

Scraps of fabric for motifs in red, green, and white plaid and red-and-white check

Scissors

Fabric glue

9 small and 4 medium-sized flat cream buttons

Dressmaking pins

Pale green sewing thread and sewing needle

Thick green and red thread and large needle

By following the instructions given here for the reindeer card, you will be able to make any of the cards shown on page 94, using the motifs given in the template library. Tags are made in much the same way, but a background fabric is glued to the stiff paper before the motifs are glued in place. After the fabric collage is complete, the tag is cut to the desired shape.

For tag ties, you can use a length of string or a narrow raw-edged strip of scrap fabric, or a narrow ribbon in a complementary color.

## MAKING A CARD

**1** Fold the rectangle of stiff white paper in half. Cut out a 5½ in (14 cm) square of calico, unravel the edge, and glue it to the center of the front of the card.

**2** From the red-and-white check fabric, cut out four 1 in (2.5 cm) squares and unravel the edges. Then glue one square in each corner of the calico.

**3** From the red-and-white plaid, cut out a 3½ in (9 cm) square and unravel the edges. Glue the square to the center of the calico.

**4** Using the reindeer template on page 127, cut the motif from calico. Then glue it to the center of the red-and-white plaid square.

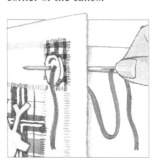

**5** Using thick green thread and a needle, attach a button to each red-and-white check corner square, securing with a knot.

**6** Make a bow of thick green thread and glue it to the reindeer's neck.

## DECORATING A PRESENT BAG

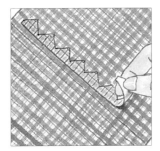

**1** Using the template on page 126, cut a zigzag strip 13½ in (34 cm) long from the red, green, and white plaid. Glue it in place across the center of the blue-and-white plaid bag fabric.

**2** Using the templates on page 127, cut eight small stars from the red-and-white check fabric and glue one in place at the tip of each zigzag point.

**3** Using the templates on page 127, cut one large star from the red-and-white check fabric and a tree from the red, green, and white plaid. Glue the tree and the star to the calico pocket piece.

**4** Fold ¾ in (2 cm) to the wrong side along the bottom and two sides of the pocket piece, then fold 1¼ in (3 cm) to the wrong side across the top of the pocket piece. Press in place.

**5** Using thick green thread, attach a medium-sized button to each pocket corner, securing with a bow. Using red thread, attach a small button to the tree star, knotting to secure.

**6** Using thick red thread and securing with a knot, attach a medium-sized button to the tip of each zigzag point.

**7** Pin the pocket to the front of the bag 1¼ in (3 cm) above the tips of the zigzag motif and sew in place using pale green sewing thread and running stitch.

**8** Sew on the casing and complete the bag as instructed on pages 30 and 31. Then thread the red and white plaid drawstring through the casings and knot each end.

# DIRECTORY & TEMPLATES

When you need instant inspiration, browse through the directory. You'll find a range of color schemes and styles, and lots more examples of the techniques and finishing touches featured in the Special Occasions section. The template library provides all the patterns and motifs needed.

# DIRECTORY
## *of*
# TECHNIQUES

When you are searching for inspiration, this quick reference directory will give you a host of ideas plus advice on which techniques are fast and easy, which can be successfully tackled by children, and which are a little more time consuming and thus more appropriate for very special occasions. It also provides an alternative design for each of the techniques described in the Special Occasions section that shows how easy it is to adapt these techniques to suit different occasions simply by altering the choice of colors and motifs.

All of the techniques can be used to create unique gift papers, tags, and cards, and to decorate envelopes, gift bags, and boxes. If you are in a hurry, some of the techniques can be used to add a personal touch to purchased gift wraps. Simply outline the pattern on store-bought paper with relief paint or add torn- or cut-paper motifs. Or you can decorate the envelope of a purchased greeting card with spattered paint or stamped patterns.

If you have more time, experiment with combining some of the techniques. The découpage and stenciled paper illustrated on page 105 will show you how effective this can be.

Motifs can be chosen from the selection of templates on pages 112–127. Or search for your own motifs in books and magazines.

For more detailed information about a specific technique, and for full instructions, turn to the accompanying page references.

### DECOUPAGE

Look in magazines to find motifs to cut out. For repeat motifs, photocopy your cutouts. You can color black and white motifs with paints, felt-tipped pens, or colored pencils as shown here. Finding appropriate motifs, cutting them out, and if necessary, duplicating them, makes this technique time consuming. Save it for very special gifts or let the kids loose on a pile of old magazines. Grandma will love the results. *See pages 60–63.*

### SPATTERED PAPER

This technique is worked by spattering paint onto paper with a toothbrush. Although you need to take care to protect your work surface, it is a quick paint technique that requires little time or effort, but provides appealing results. Even young children can join in the fun. *See page 36.*

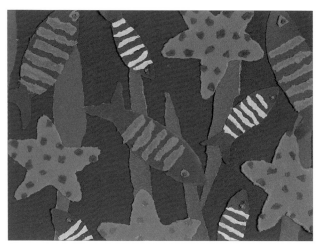

## PIERCED PAPER

This ingenious decoration is produced by using a needle to pierce patterns into the paper. The effect achieved depends on the size of the holes, the paper texture and color, and the intricacy or simplicity of the motifs. Try a tag or card first before you tackle a whole sheet of paper.
*See pages 42–43.*

## TORN PAPER

A few scraps of torn paper can personalize a store-bought item very quickly. Add torn paper to gift wrap, boxes, tags, and envelopes. You can also use this technique to create an elaborate collage effect that the recipient will want to frame and keep.
*See pages 78–79.*

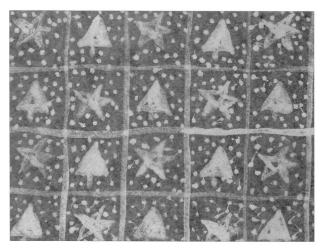

## CUT PAPER

Wrapping a present with plain paper and decorating the paper with cut-paper motifs and ready-made stickers is the perfect way to personalize a gift. Young children can add store-bought stickers while older ones will be able to cut out and glue on motifs that fit the occasion and recipient. Remember cut-paper motifs and stickers look great on envelopes too.
*See pages 54–55.*

## BLEACHED PAPER

Painting tissue paper with a weak bleach solution creates a delightful and unique gift paper. The technique is quick and easy to execute when simple motifs are chosen. Bleach should always be kept away from young children, but older ones will enjoy experimenting with this unusual technique.
*See pages 72–73.*

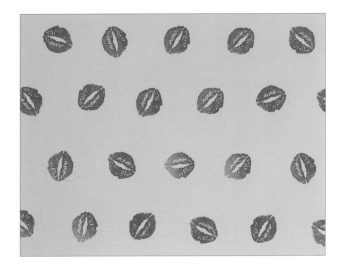

## STAMPED PAPER

The simplest of all the decorative techniques, stamping is ideal for children. It will add just that touch of handmade charm without taking too much time. Stamps are very popular and are available in a vast array of sizes and designs, or you can make your own unique stamps using shapes cut from fruit and vegetables.
*See pages 84–85.*

## DRY-BRUSH MOTIFS

This type of stenciling is achieved by using the paint sparingly and applying it with a stiff, dry brush. It produces an attractive folk-art look and it is impossible to get wrong; any imperfections are part of the charm. You can work very quickly and create paper and matching cards and tags.
*See pages 90–91.*

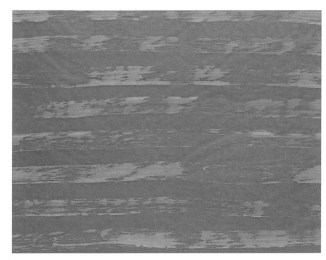

## STENCILING

Used as wall and furniture decoration, stenciling is also a stylish technique for gift paper. The motifs are applied by dabbing paint into a cut-out stencil template. Cut your own templates or choose from the wide range available in stores. Select motifs to suit the recipient or occasion.
*See pages 66–67.*

## DRY-BRUSH PATTERNS

Dry-brush patterns can be rustled up in a few minutes if you are in a hurry to get your gift ready for the party. And because you use very little paint, this is not a messy technique to use if you already have your party clothes on. The end result should have a simple, rustic feel. Don't strive for perfection.
*See page 37.*

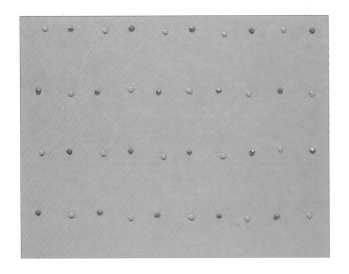

## RELIEF-PAINT DOTS

Nothing could be easier than applying dots of plastic relief paint to paper to dress it up. The effect will suit every occasion. By varying the spacing of the dots and the colors of gift paper and paint, you can achieve subtly different creations. Relief paint is also perfect for highlighting patterns on store-bought paper and cards to add an individual touch.
*See page 37.*

## CHALKED PAPER

Chalk designs are created by using the side edge or the tip of a piece of chalk. The soft colors and textures of the chalk lines ensure a captivating effect, and once it is sprayed with a fixative, the design won't smudge.
*See pages 48–49.*

## FABRIC COLLAGE

Pasting fabric shapes onto paper creates a gift paper for a very special present. This collage technique is also ideal for making memorable tags and greeting cards. Use the same technique on fabric if you are sewing a gift bag or stocking and want to add motifs to suit the occasion.
*See pages 98–99.*

## COMBINED DECOUPAGE AND STENCILING

By combining two or three decorative paper techniques, you can expand the design possibilities even more. The paper above combines découpage dogs and stenciled bones, but endless other combinations will come to mind.
*See pages 60–61 for découpage instructions and pages 66–67 for stenciling instructions.*

# DIRECTORY *of* FINISHING TOUCHES

Thoughtful finishing touches needn't take much time, but they can transform a gift and give great pleasure to the recipient. For one of the simplest yet most striking touches, tuck one or two fresh flowers or a tiny posy beneath the ribbon on a gift. Fresh leaves, including bay and ivy, can also be used to great effect.

When your gift has to be left wrapped for some time and fresh flowers aren't appropriate, there are many attractive alternatives. Look for acorns, fir cones, and seed pods that can be used to decorate a gift, or make tiny posies from dried flowers and grasses. Gilded berries and leaves are perfect for winter birthdays and Christmas gifts.

Flowers can also be made simply and quickly from ribbon or paper and used either singly or in tiny bunches.

Bows are the traditional finishing touch for presents and this directory gives you a delightful choice of styles. Remember that ribbon is just one possible choice for a bow: string, wool, raffia, and fabric are just a few of the alternatives.

Tags are especially important as they carry your message to the recipient. They make perfect keepsakes, and Christmas tags can be hung on the tree year after year. Many of the tags shown here can also be glued to cardboard to make a card.

For more details about a specific finishing touch, and for full instructions, turn to the accompanying page references.

## FLOWERS, LEAVES, AND BERRIES

### FRESH FLOWERS
*Bright, colorful flowers are a perfect finishing touch.*

### FRESH FLOWER POSY
*Tie together tiny flowers and leaves. Scented flowers are ideal.*

### FRESH LEAVES
*Ivy, bay, and holly make great finishing touches.*

### NATURAL DECORATIONS
*Use fir cones, acorns, feathers, and other found objects for decoration.*

## DRIED FLOWER POSY

*Tie together tiny dried flowers and grasses.*

## RIBBON ROSES

*See page 22.*

## GILDED DECORATIONS

*See page 38.*

## PAPER SPRING FLOWERS

*See pages 74 and 75.*

## GILDED POSY

*Tie berries and leaves in a tiny posy and see page 38 for gilding instructions.*

## PAPER ROSES

*See page 68.*

## DECORATED PRESSED AND PAPER LEAVES

*See page 39.*

## PAPER ROSE POSY

*See page 69.*

# BOWS AND TIES

### WIRE-EDGED RIBBON BOW
*Tie as for basic bow, page 19.*

### TWISTED-PAPER RIBBON BOW
*See page 21.*

### PAPER-STRING BOW
*See page 80 for instructions on making crepe paper string. Put different colored strands together and tie as for basic bow, page 19.*

### RAFFIA BOW
*See page 20.*

### CUT-END BOW
*See page 23.*

### FINE-RIBBON BOW WITH TRAILERS
*See page 21.*

### STRING BOW
*Tie as for basic bow, page 19.*

### NET BOW
*Tie as for basic bow (page 19). Can be filled with confetti (page 44).*

## GROSGRAIN BOW

*Tie as for basic bow, page 19.*

## CREPE-PAPER BOW

*Cut a strip of crepe paper and tie as for basic bow, page 19.*

## FABRIC BOW

*Cut a strip of non-fraying fabric and tie as for basic bow, page 19.*

## BOW WITH TRAILERS

*Certain types of synthetic ribbon can be curled using a blunt-edged knife or the side of a pair of scissors. See page 73 for instructions.*

## PUNCHED-PAPER BOW

*For punching holes in paper, see pages 54 and 55. For bow instructions, follow the steps for the fine-ribbon bow on page 21, omitting the trailers.*

## CUT-END STRING BOW

*See page 23 for instructions, but use thin string instead of raffia.*

## EMBELLISHED BOW

*See page 22.*

## CREPE-PAPER TIE

*Make crepe-paper string following the instructions on page 80, tie it on the gift, then knot a strip of crepe paper across to form a bow.*

# GIFT TAGS

**FABRIC COLLAGE TAG**
*See page 98.*

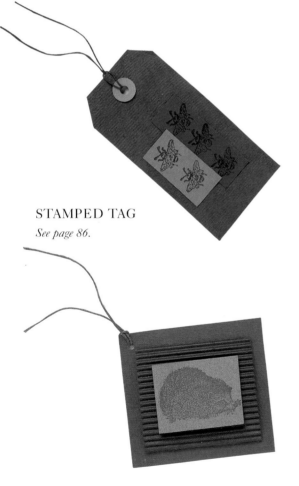

**STAMPED TAG**
*See page 86.*

**STAMPED 3-D TAG**
*See page 87.*

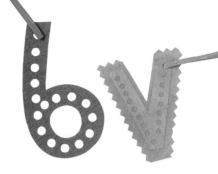

**NUMBER AND LETTER TAGS**
*See pages 56 and 57.*

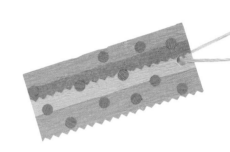

**CUT-PAPER TAG**
*See page 54.*

**TORN-PAPER TAG**
*See page 79.*

**PIERCED-PAPER TAG**
*See page 42.*

## STENCILED TAG
*See page 66.*

## CHALKED TAG WITH MOTIF
*See page 50.*

## QUICK PAINT TECHNIQUE SHAPED TAG
*See page 92.*

## DECOUPAGE TISSUE-COVERED TAG
*See page 63.*

## SPRING FLOWER TAG
*See page 75.*

## DECOUPAGE AND TORN-TISSUE TAG
*See page 63.*

## CHALKED TAG
*See page 50.*

## SHAPED DECOUPAGE PARCEL
*See page 62 for découpage and page 93 for parcel instructions.*

111

# TEMPLATE LIBRARY

Where templates are needed for items in this book they are given on the following pages. Templates that you will want to use in various sizes, such as envelopes, and the alphabet and number motifs, are shown on grid lines.

The quickest way to duplicate a template at the same size as it is shown in the library is by photocopying it. Cut out the photocopied image and use it as a pattern to cut or draw around.

For complex designs, such as the wedding tag template on page 116, or if you do not have access to a photocopier, you can transfer a design using tracing paper. Place tracing paper over the template and trace the outline using a hard-lead pencil. Turn the tracing paper over and lay it on scrap paper. Go back and forth over the traced outline with a soft-lead pencil. Turn the tracing paper over, lay it on thin cardboard (for a template) or your card, tag or wrapping paper as appropriate, and draw over the motif outline. A copy of the outline will then be reproduced on your cardboard or paper.

Using a photocopier that can enlarge or reduce an image is the quickest way of making templates larger or smaller. If you don't have access to a photocopier with this facility, use the grid method to alter the size of the template. The grid lines given in the template library are ½ in (1.25 cm) apart. So if you want to make the template twice the size shown, draw the outline of the template on 1 in (2.5 cm) grid paper, copying it across square by square. Notice the points where the outline crosses the lines of the original grid and make sure that it crosses the corresponding lines of your own grid. If you want to make the template half the size shown, use grid paper with divisions ¼ in (6 mm) apart.

## ENVELOPES

### SIMPLE ENVELOPE

This template will make an envelope 3½ x 2¼ in (9 x 6 cm). To make an envelope 7 x 4½ in (18 x 12 cm), which is the size of the envelope photographed for this book, enlarge to 200 percent on a photocopier or copy onto 1 in (2.5 cm) grid paper. Foldlines are marked by broken lines. See page 24 for instructions on how to assemble.

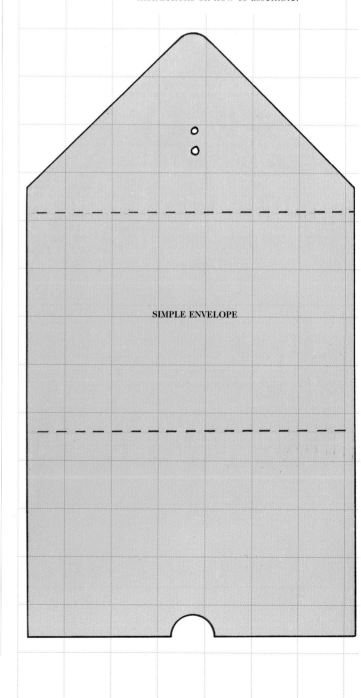

SIMPLE ENVELOPE

### ENVELOPE WITH FLAPS

This template will make an envelope 3½ x 2½ in (9 x 6.5 cm). To make an envelope 7 x 5 in (18 x 13 cm), which is the size of the envelope photographed for this book, enlarge to 200 percent on a photocopier or copy onto 1 in (2.5 cm) grid paper. Foldlines are marked by broken lines. See page 25 for instructions on how to assemble.

### WALLET ENVELOPE

This template will make an envelope 2½ x 2¾ in (6.5 x 7 cm). To make an envelope 5 x 5½ in (13 x 14 cm), which is the size of the envelope photographed for this book, enlarge to 200 percent on a photocopier or copy onto 1 in (2.5 cm) grid paper. Foldlines are marked by broken lines. See page 25 for instructions on how to assemble.

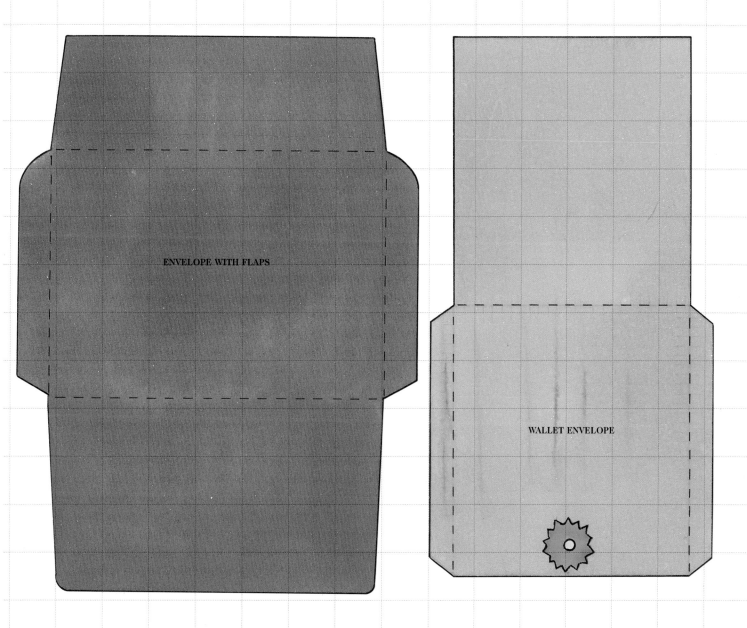

ENVELOPE WITH FLAPS

WALLET ENVELOPE

# BOX, FLATPACK, CONE, AND TAGS

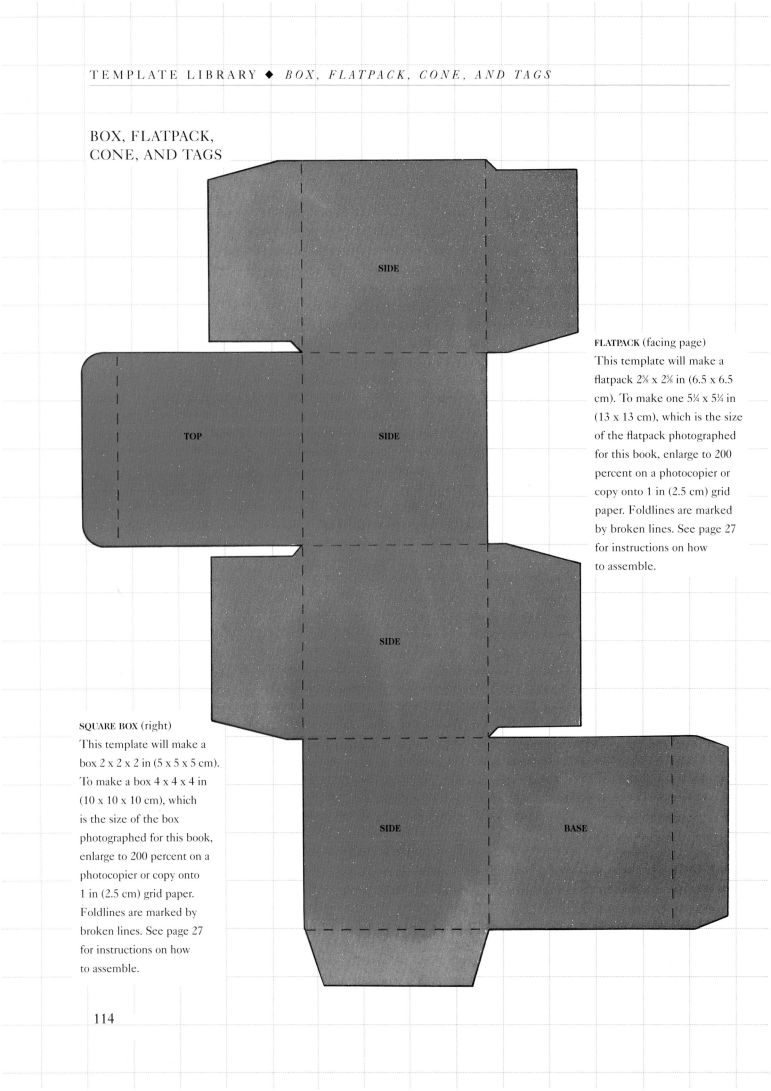

**FLATPACK** (facing page)
This template will make a
flatpack 2⅝ x 2⅝ in (6.5 x 6.5
cm). To make one 5¼ x 5¼ in
(13 x 13 cm), which is the size
of the flatpack photographed
for this book, enlarge to 200
percent on a photocopier or
copy onto 1 in (2.5 cm) grid
paper. Foldlines are marked
by broken lines. See page 27
for instructions on how
to assemble.

**SQUARE BOX** (right)
This template will make a
box 2 x 2 x 2 in (5 x 5 x 5 cm).
To make a box 4 x 4 x 4 in
(10 x 10 x 10 cm), which
is the size of the box
photographed for this book,
enlarge to 200 percent on a
photocopier or copy onto
1 in (2.5 cm) grid paper.
Foldlines are marked by
broken lines. See page 27
for instructions on how
to assemble.

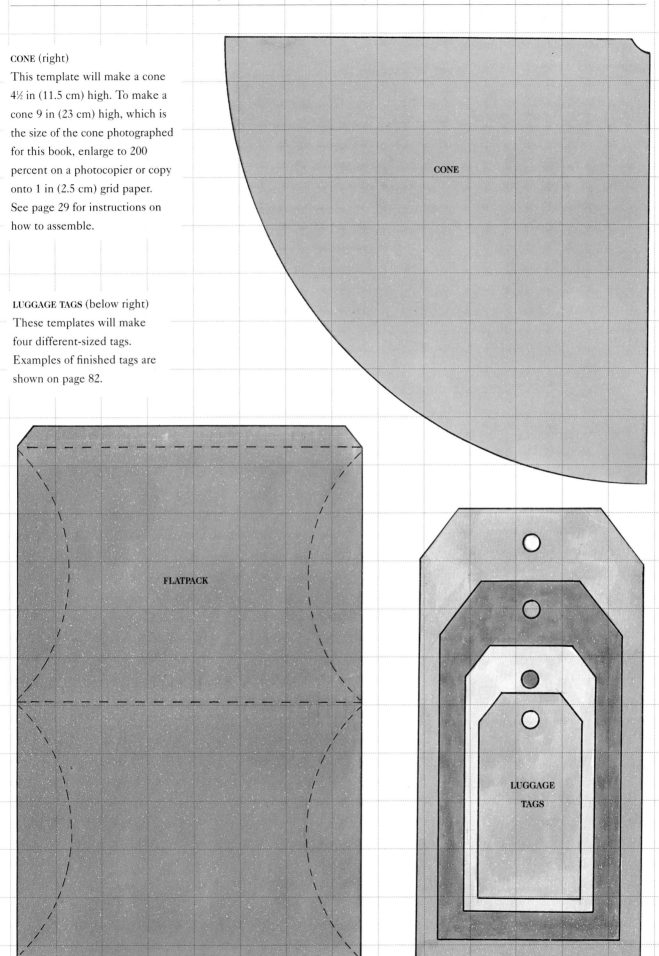

CONE (right)

This template will make a cone
4½ in (11.5 cm) high. To make a
cone 9 in (23 cm) high, which is
the size of the cone photographed
for this book, enlarge to 200
percent on a photocopier or copy
onto 1 in (2.5 cm) grid paper.
See page 29 for instructions on
how to assemble.

CONE

LUGGAGE TAGS (below right)

These templates will make
four different-sized tags.
Examples of finished tags are
shown on page 82.

FLATPACK

LUGGAGE
TAGS

## CONGRATULATIONS

**PAPER LEAF MOTIFS**
(below and right)
See page 39 for instructions
on decorating these.

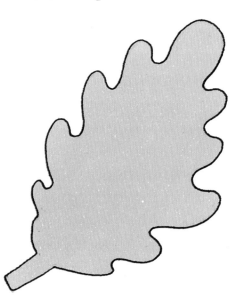

## WEDDING

**PIERCED-PAPER
HEART MOTIFS**
(right and facing page)
Heart motifs with designs
suitable for paper piercing.
The three largest hearts
(right and facing page) are
suitable for making gift tags
and cards. The two smaller
hearts (facing page) can be
used for repetitive designs
on paper or for creating
borders to cards and tags.
See pages 42 and 43 for
instructions.

# WEDDING

### PIERCED-PAPER TAG OR CARD (right)

For a small card or tag, use template at the size shown. To make a card the size of the one photographed for this book, enlarge to 200 percent using a photocopier or the grid method explained on page 112. See pages 42 and 43 for instructions.

### PIERCED GIFT PAPER (below)

This shows the arrangement of hearts used in the pierced paper project on pages 42 and 43. Trace one of these hearts to make a template for this project.

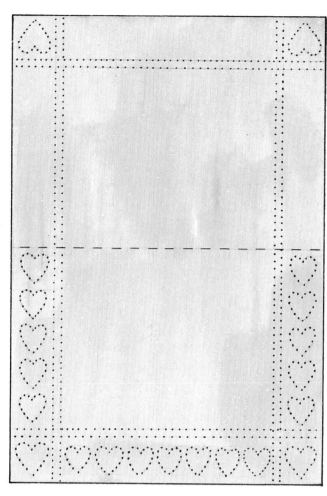

## NEW BABY

**CHAIN DOLLS**
Note that chain
motifs are joined
at the hands.
See page 51 for
instructions on
how to make
chain motifs.

**CHAIN BUNNIES**
Note the bunnies are joined
at the tail. See page 51 for
instructions on how to make
chain motifs.

**TAG MOTIFS**
Bunny (right) and bird
(far right). See page 50 for
instructions.

118

# CHILD'S BIRTHDAY

**ALPHABET AND
NUMBER MOTIFS**
See pages 56 and 57 for
instructions on making
cut-paper tags and cards.
To enlarge or reduce these
templates, use a photo-
copier or the grid method
explained on page 112.

A B C
D E F G H
I J K L M
N O P Q

## CHILD'S BIRTHDAY    ALPHABET AND NUMBER MOTIFS

# RSTUV
# WXYZ
# 12345
# 67890

# VALENTINE'S DAY

**ROSE AND LEAF**
**STENCIL MOTIFS**
Rose (far right) and rose leaf
(right). See page 66 and 67 for
instructions on how to cut a
stencil and use it to decorate
gift paper, and page 64 for a
finished example.

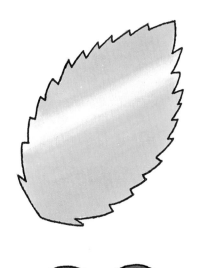

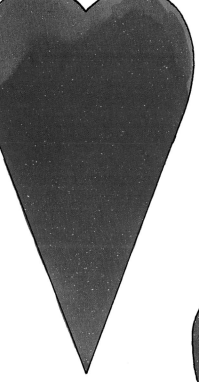

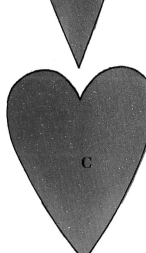

**HEART STENCIL MOTIFS**
You can choose the size and
shape of heart motif that
best suits your project from
the variety of heart motifs
shown here. The heart motifs
used in the projects on pages
66 and 67 are labeled as
follows:
A is used to make the tag and
B and C are used to make
stencils to decorate gift paper.

## VALENTINE'S DAY

**PAPER ROSE TEMPLATES**
See pages 68 and 69 for
how to make the rose.

Section C is the beginning (right-hand end) of the rose template, section B the middle, and section A the end (left-hand). For the large rose, trace A, then add B 9 times, then add C. Use this pattern to cut out your rose. (See small plan of rose, below actual-size templates, for guidance.) For the rosebud, trace A, then add B 7 times, then add C.

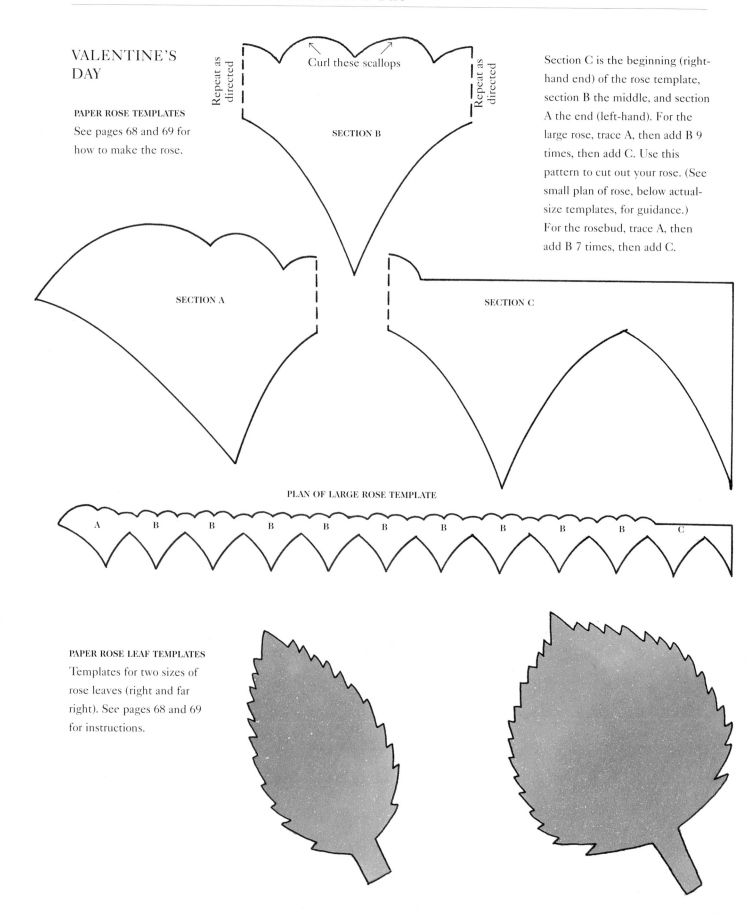

Repeat as directed

Curl these scallops

SECTION B

Repeat as directed

SECTION A

SECTION C

PLAN OF LARGE ROSE TEMPLATE

A B B B B B B B B C

**PAPER ROSE LEAF TEMPLATES**
Templates for two sizes of
rose leaves (right and far
right). See pages 68 and 69
for instructions.

# EASTER

**YELLOW PAPER FLOWER**
Use the petal shapes (right), the stem template (center right), and the leaves if required (far right). For instructions see page 74.

**DAISY PAPER FLOWER**
Use the daisy motif (below) and tag bases (below right) to make the daisy tag or card. For instructions see page 75.

# MOTHER'S DAY AND EASTER

**SCALLOPED FLOWERS**
Use the scalloped templates (right or far right) for torn-paper flowers on pages 78 and 79. These templates can also be used to make small single flowers for Easter, see page 70 for finished results.

YELLOW PAPER
FLOWER SHAPES

LEAF SHAPES

STEM SHAPE

DAISY MOTIF

TAG BASES

SCALLOPED FLOWER
MOTIFS

SIMPLE SCALLOPED
FLOWER MOTIF

## TRADITIONAL CHRISTMAS

**LARGE STAR SHAPE** (right)
This motif can be used to make a shaped package or tag. See pages 92 and 93 for instructions.

**STAR STENCIL MOTIFS**
Two stars (right and below). See page 66 for cutting a stencil and pages 90 and 91 for instructions on decorating a box with dry-brushed stenciled stars.

**CHRISTMAS TREE WITH STAR MOTIF** (below)
See page 93 for instructions on how to make a tree-shaped package.

## TRADITIONAL CHRISTMAS

**TEMPLATES FOR SHAPED PACKAGES**
The large holly (right), angel (below right), and ornament (bottom) are for shaped packages. See page 93 for instructions.

**SHAPED TAG OR STENCIL**
The small holly (below) can be used for a shaped tag or for dry-brush stenciling. See pages 92, and pages 90 and 91 for instructions.

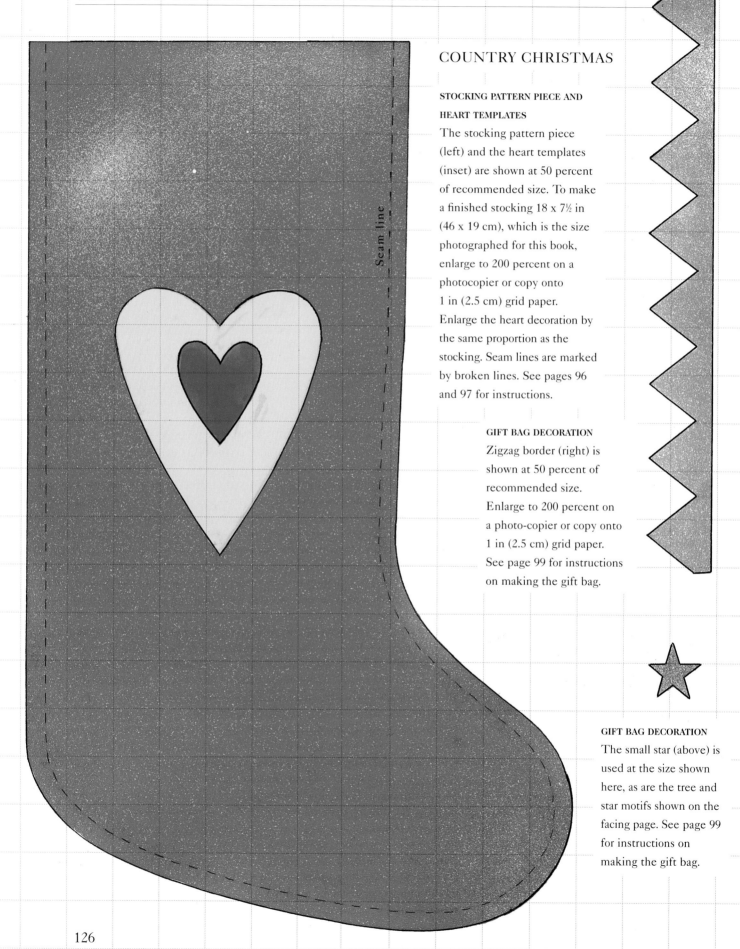

Seam line

## COUNTRY CHRISTMAS

**STOCKING PATTERN PIECE AND
HEART TEMPLATES**
The stocking pattern piece
(left) and the heart templates
(inset) are shown at 50 percent
of recommended size. To make
a finished stocking 18 x 7½ in
(46 x 19 cm), which is the size
photographed for this book,
enlarge to 200 percent on a
photocopier or copy onto
1 in (2.5 cm) grid paper.
Enlarge the heart decoration by
the same proportion as the
stocking. Seam lines are marked
by broken lines. See pages 96
and 97 for instructions.

**GIFT BAG DECORATION**
Zigzag border (right) is
shown at 50 percent of
recommended size.
Enlarge to 200 percent on
a photo-copier or copy onto
1 in (2.5 cm) grid paper.
See page 99 for instructions
on making the gift bag.

**GIFT BAG DECORATION**
The small star (above) is
used at the size shown
here, as are the tree and
star motifs shown on the
facing page. See page 99
for instructions on
making the gift bag.

## COUNTRY CHRISTMAS

**HEART MOTIF** (below)
Use for cards, tags, or as an alternative decoration for the gift bag. See instructions on pages 96 to 99.

**STAR MOTIFS** (right)
Star A is for a gift bag, and stars B and C for cards and tags. See page 99 for gift bag instructions and page 94 for finished item. Star D is for the large tree below.

**REINDEER MOTIF** (below)
See page 98 for instructions on making a fabric-collage card.

**TREE MOTIFS** (right)
The largest tree is used to decorate the gift bag, see page 99. The two smaller trees can be used for cards, tags, or alternative decorations for the present bag or stocking.